BATTLES

MY JOURNEY OF
SELF & SERVICE

WITHIN

★ ★ ★

ADAM D. DEMARCO

Ballast Books, LLC
www.ballastbooks.com

Copyright © 2023 by Adam D. DeMarco

ISBN 9781955026406

Published by Ballast Books
www.ballastbooks.com

For more information, bulk orders, appearances or speaking requests, please email info@ballastbooks.com

This book is written for those who have ventured off the straight and narrow. For those who have taken the road less traveled. It's for the people that have stood up for what they believed in, even if that meant standing alone. It's for those who have dared mighty things and been met with both victory and defeat. And this is for those who in the face of nearly insurmountable odds have the courage to continue the mission, their mission.

"Charlie Mike."

CONTENTS

Chapter 1

FOUNDATIONS

There's a story that my dad loves to tell. When I was a little kid, growing up in the outskirts of Washington, DC, we were at a park with my best friend Aaron and his parents. Something happened and sent my young friend, we were both around three years old, into a meltdown. He came running back to his parents crying that some other kids were being mean—playground bullies. I, ever the defender, rose from my juice box in my overalls and, with the bold conviction that only a toddler could possess, defiantly told Aaron, "Show me where they are. I'll take care of them." What happened next isn't important, nor memorable. And while it's a relatively silly story, which probably elicits more laughs or sighs, it is probably the first representation of who I am, and who I hoped to become.

I was born in Baltimore, Maryland, smack dab in the most beautiful time of year for the Mid-Atlantic-Chesapeake region: October 1985. My first few years were spent living along the Baltimore-Washington Parkway, a stone's throw from a popular outdoor music venue called Merriweather Post Pavilion, the same place that Jackson Browne live recorded one of my favorite songs, "The Load-Out," in 1977.

My dad and I have always had a very special bond. And he has certainly carried a lot of titles—dad, coach, scout den leader, mentor, friend—but I think the most accurate and complete title is hero. He was a former law enforcement officer who then worked in the federal government, before later returning to the Florida Department of Law Enforcement, which was the catalyst for our family to move to Florida.

My mom was a property manager, mainly for apartment complexes, which means that I was raised in and grew up in apartments for nearly my entire life. For a kid, it was great. There's always a pool, other kids to play with, and the ever-present opportunity to get into some trouble.

When we first moved to Florida, we lived in Broward County, but my parents were able to get me enrolled in a private Catholic school in the affluent area of Boca Raton called St. Jude. I would spend my days going to school with kids whose parents were some of the wealthiest people in the region, and at night I'd be playing soccer and baseball with kids who lived on food stamps: the tale of two worlds.

Playing soccer during that time, I was invited to play on the "travel team." Which meant that I would spend nearly every weekend traveling across southern Florida, from Coral Springs to Kendall to Miami Lakes, playing rather competitive games against kids my age but from a whole different world. I remember many of them spoke little to no English, and for some, they had just arrived in America only a few short months or years ago. I had no idea what immigration was back then, nor did I see my teammates and opposing players as immigrants. They were just kids, and we were all playing the game we loved. And I think that's the beauty of the innocence of childhood.

Even to this day, my mom talks of how happy a kid I was, and to an extent, a fearless trendsetter. Did I take gymnastics? Yes. Did

I sign up for the school talent show to play the song "We Will Rock You" on the drum set I got for Christmas? Absolutely. Did I know how to play the drums? Hell no. Yet while my earliest memories should be of playing soccer and eating oranges, summers spent at Disney World, or road trips to West Virginia with my grandma, many of my earliest memories from that time are overshadowed by an ever-present cloud.

I can't remember the kid's name, but I remember he was much older. I was five, and he was maybe nine or ten. Even though I was in kindergarten, we both would be at after-school day care, and our working parents would come get us after school let out. At this point as a child, my ears had grown much faster than the rest of me and stuck out a bit. The medical term for this is "protruding" or "prominent," and while there are no adverse physical health effects, being a young kid with big ears certainly had psychological ones. And for a five-year-old, this was the end of the world.

For nearly a year in kindergarten, I was teased and harassed to the point that I came home in tears every day from school. I was called every name in the book, but Dumbo was the worst. Once a happy, bright, vibrant kid, I had been verbally beaten down and bullied to the point that my parents did everything they could to ease this childhood trauma.

After several interventions from my parents and the school, the bullying stopped, thankfully. But the invisible scars remained. Anyone who says trite expressions like "words don't matter, actions do" or the adage "sticks and stones may break my bones, but words will never hurt me" has never been on the receiving end of bullying to this extent, especially as a child.

This may sound surprising to most, as this is not something that I actively share, but the summer after kindergarten, my parents—trying to salvage the spirit of a beaten and bullied kid—decided that maybe surgery would ease my pain and instill me with the confidence that was stripped from me. The surgery is called otoplasty and is a simple routine outpatient procedure. Basically, a doctor cuts your ear and with sutures "pins them back," thereby reducing the protrusion or, as I called it, my "Dumbo ears." And while I have no idea if the surgery made any long-term difference, what I do know is that for that five-year-old kid who came home crying every day from school because of constant bullying, knowing that I looked like everyone else again made all the difference. The wounds inflicted by my childhood bullies were stitched shut, but the scars would certainly remain.

Years later, our family moved to the Gulf Coast of Florida, Sarasota to be exact, which was a 180-degree turn from my growing up on the East Coast of Florida. Trading in the collared shirt and penny loafers of Catholic school for the newest trends of public middle school was a shock, but only to be eclipsed by the feeling of being the new kid—a small fish in a big pond. Anyone who has ever been the new kid in school knows that you immediately have both a spotlight on your face and a target on your back. And that was certainly the case for me.

Friends were usually easy for me to make as a kid, but mostly because of association and convenience versus connection. Playing competitive soccer put me in a rather exclusive club of traveling around the country with a select group of kids and families, staying in hotels, spending holidays at local truck stop restaurants, and having lots of motel pool birthday parties. The same could be said for my time in Catholic school, where I essentially grew up with the same twenty kids since kindergarten. But now, I was out in the wild.

Being the new kid coupled with the overall awkwardness of the middle school years, exacerbated only by the male challenges of puberty, made me an instant target. I didn't know where I fit in. I was athletic but smart. I was a troublemaker but kind. And I was terrible with girls but—as my soon-to-be best friend Brady would say— "they digged me."

At the age of thirteen, Brady was a hulking six-foot-four inch, 250-pound football player. He was a transplant from elsewhere as well and knew the troubles of being the new kid. We would jokingly say that our friendship was a mixture between the hilariously underrated movie *Twins*, starring Arnold Schwarzenegger and Danny DeVito, and the young adult novel *Freak the Mighty*. Only years later would I find out that the main reason he befriended me was because the girls in my grade gave me all the attention. I guess big ears and blue eyes do have their perks after all.

Brady and I would be inseparable for nearly the next decade. A perfectly odd couple. We would experience the highs and lows of teenage life and angst together. Never quite in the cool crowd but never the outcasts. Safely in the middle.

Our friendship solidified into a brotherly bond that took us from the playgrounds and sports fields of middle school to summer camps, and then eventually to the battleground that is high school. Riverview High School to be exact.

Legend has it that Sarasota was named after famed Spanish conquistador Hernando de Soto's daughter, Sara, but the real development of the southwest Florida city occurred in the late 1800s because of investments from Scottish companies. Therefore, Riverview High School not only took on the ram as a mascot as a nod to the Scottish heritage but also outfitted the entire band in traditional tartans and kilts, complete with bagpipers and highland dancers. So, if you didn't come to the Ram Bowl for football, as was often the case, you came for an incredible show including a bagpipe rendition of "Amazing Grace" and the traditional Scottish sword dance.

Navigating high school was easy. Probably because of the scar tissue of my childhood bullying, I wasn't really phased by the goons, and there were certainly a lot of them. Riverview High School was a school right out of central casting for a terrible early 2000s movie starring Freddie Prinze Jr. We had jocks and jerks, stoners, smart kids, troublemakers, and two-good-for-you preppies. My best friend Brady and I, together, rode the seams between each group and never really took membership in one or the other. Some would say we were well rounded, but looking back, I think it, I, was intuitively political.

Brady and I also tried out for the freshman football team. He had played football before and I hadn't—my mom wouldn't let me—so when it came to the difficult task of figuring out how to put shoulder pads on or how to buckle my helmet, Brady was the sole reason I didn't show up to practice looking like an idiot.

I caught onto football quickly. Granted I was maybe five foot seven, a hundred and twenty pounds soaking wet, I wanted to play safety and defensive back to emulate my favorite players, namely Tampa Bay Buccaneer John Lynch. Brady was a tight end; he could move and had great hands, making the perfect tight end. And while I rode the bench for the entire year—yes, I never played a single down—I did have two practice "highlights" that would be ingrained in my memory. The first isn't so much of a highlight but more of a lesson. I was lined up against Frank Young, a strong kid who could play nearly every position and excelled at each one equally, in what's called the "Oklahoma drill."

"Oklahoma" is a one-versus-one test of grit, strength, and toughness and, for us boys of summer, a rite of passage. Frank was on offense and was running the ball, and I was on defense. Starting on our backs, the coach blew the whistle, and we both got up as fast as we could with my goal to stop the runner and his goal to get past me. Well, it was that day on the swampy banks that I learned through the application of Newton's second law of motion that force equals mass times acceleration and was summarily steamrolled by Frank. I had been in playground scuffles before and involved in minor collisions on the soccer field, but that was the first time that I ever had the lights go out. Like with a first kiss, you never forget the first time you have your clock absolutely cleaned eight ways from Sunday.

Getting up, a bit disoriented and more than likely with a concussion, I learned a valuable lesson that day. Aside from experiencing the genius of Sir Isaac Newton firsthand, as the rest of the team was hooting and hollering, I could have just lain there until their cheers simmered and a trainer ran over to check on me. But instead, I got back up, albeit a bit wobbly, but under my own power and agency. And it is that day I learned that when you get the shit kicked out of you, there isn't much you can do about it, except make the decision to get right back up. We have very little control over most things that will happen to us in life. However, what we can control is how we react to them. As Rocky Balboa put so perfectly, "It ain't about how hard you can hit. It's about how hard you can get hit and keep moving forward."

The second highlight from that miserable year of freshman football is when as a third- or fourth-string safety on defense, I went in against the first-string offense. Assuming the play was going to be a run, I cheated up a bit from the normal depth at which a safety would line up. As I was the low man on the totem, I knew that if I made one big play, I could catch the coach's eye and move up from my tertiary position on the depth chart.

The ball was hiked, and I took my several read steps back only to then see the quarterback drop back, and the tight end move downfield instead of pull, meaning that the tight end was running a passing route instead of looking for a block. I followed him as he moved across the field, from my left to right, on what looked like a slant route. I saw in my periphery the quarterback laser focused on the tight end and deliver a wobbly duck of a pass to him. The tight end caught it, secured it, and turned up field to run for a touchdown. Except, I was right in the way of this moving locomotive, ready to be crushed.

I squared up with the monstrous tight end, and having learned from my first highlight, I got as low as I could to not feel the full brunt of the force of this beastly mass barreling toward me. I remembered he lowered his shoulder pads, and the last thing I saw was the football as I lined my helmet up with it, as we were taught. I then closed my eyes and hoped for the best.

When I opened my eyes back up after the collision and heard the whistle, everyone was cheering. I immediately thought, "Shit... not again." Except this time everyone was coming up and hitting me on the helmet. Apparently, my leverage coupled with the perfect helmet-to-ball contact forced the tight end to fumble the ball, and the scraps of the last-string defense just caused a turnover against the first-string offense, a big deal back then. My coaches were ecstatic. The other coaches, not so much. The offensive coaches began to lambast the guy who fumbled. You haven't been truly cussed out until you've been cussed out by a southern high school football coach.

I watched in amusement as the player jogged off to the side, getting ripped into the whole way, and then as he took his helmet off, I realized that it was my best friend, Brady, who I just forced to fumble. I couldn't wait until after practice to talk shit to him.

In the locker room, I went over and began to heckle him. But to my unfortunate realization, it was immediately apparent that he didn't find the situation as funny as I did. In fact, he was pissed. Not at me, but at himself. He felt like he had let the team down. And it was at that point that I realized this incredibly important life lesson: humility.

I could have continued to jeer Brady about the practice and gloat about the play. Except that would have had zero productive value. Yes, I would have gotten a rise and a laugh out if it, but at what expense? Whether it was young emotional intelligence or just not wanting to feel the wrath of a "Brady beat down," I realized that continuing to rib him would do nothing of value for either one of us. It was an important lesson at an important time, and one that has certainly morphed and solidified over the years: when engaged in a zero-sum game, do not add on to the thrill of victory or the sorrow of defeat through self-aggrandizement.

Looking back at those days, I sometimes laugh at just how blissfully ignorant and innocent we all were. And I guess, knowing what I know now, that sentiment was more prevalent than just in the Riverview High School freshman football team. It was a sentiment that permeated across our school, our city, hell our entire county. It wasn't just that we were young and carefree high school kids, but there was a feeling of near invincibility in those days. It's hard to think back at how quickly everything changed. Our lives and the entire American way of life—the world—were changed because of one fateful morning.

Chapter 2

OUR WORLD TURNED UPSIDE DOWN

It was the second period, and I was sitting in Mr. Marvin's biology class. I was probably daydreaming about what my life in college was going to be like, the parties, the girls, anything other than the topic at hand. It was a Tuesday, so only a couple of days left until Friday's football game. It was a home game that week, which meant that the week would be filled with pregame activities, pep rallies, and all the other cliches you can imagine associated with high school football in Florida. I was a sophomore now and had been called up from the junior varsity to the varsity team—a big deal for a fifteen-year-old.

Class was wrapping up, which was good for me because I had just about all I could take on the topic of mitochondria and adenosine triphosphate, when Mr. Mocherman unexpectedly walked into the room. He was another teacher of mine for a course I took called Nuclear Radiation; and, yes, it was just as cool as it sounds. I distinctly remember him walking over to Mr. Marvin, paying no attention to the twenty-something detached sophomores in the perfectly symmetrical rows in front. Then Mr. Marvin, a very dry guy who never let his personality show and certainly never deviated from the course syllabus, went over to the television, and turned on the local news. I couldn't see it perfectly from across the room, but it looked like something was on fire from the large black plume of smoke. And from the large buildings surrounding the billowing smoke, I could tell it wasn't in Sarasota, but then the intercom bell rang, so I grabbed my books and headed out for my next class. It was September 11, 2001.

Walking into my World History class, I saw the television was turned on to the same images of black smoke. And now I could see clearly. It was New York City, and the news chyron read "Plane Crashes into World Trade Center." As our class got settled, we continued to watch the footage, and as our teacher began collecting our homework from the night before, there was a large gasp. It wasn't a scream or a cry, but a gasp. We all turned our attention back to the television to see what occurred. It was another explosion. Another plane had hit the other tower. And we just saw it happen on live television.

At this same time, six miles away, at Emma E. Booker Elementary School, President George W. Bush was meeting with Kay Daniels, a second-grade teacher, and sixteen of her students. The president was in Sarasota to visit the school promoting the president's signature "No Child Left Behind Act." Then in a scene captured by White House photographers and videographers, White House Chief of Staff Andy Card quietly walked up to the president and whispered in his ear, "A second plane hit the second tower. America is under attack."

The rest of the day was a bit of a blur. I just remember having this sickening feeling and this overwhelming sense of helplessness and hopelessness. The syllabus of every class that day was thrown out the window. This was before the advent of smartphones and near instantaneous news cycles, so every class was spent glued to the classroom televisions. And while I didn't know what happened, or what was happening, for some reason I knew that life, my life, our American life, was never going to be the same. And I was right. Because that morning, the world was turned upside down.

In the following days of 9/11, I, like nearly every American, stayed glued to the television. I sat with my parents in our apartment fixated on the coverage of smoldering ruins. Everything else seemed so insignificant at that point. While my parents would go to bed, I would stay awake for hours. One night, I remember just listening to the Moby song "Why Does My Heart Feel So Bad" on endless repeat as I clicked through the most recent Associated Press photos from Ground Zero. Unable to sleep and helpless to do anything, I was numb. Granted I was only fifteen, but I felt like I had aged decades in those waning days and wished that there was something, anything, I could do.

Meanwhile, in the following days, members of Joint Special Operations Command (JSOC) began covert and clandestine operations to hunt and kill those responsible for the attacks on our homeland. Under the Authorization for Use of Military Force (AUMF), passed by the United States Congress and signed into law on September 18, 2001, President Bush was given near carte blanche to "use all necessary and appropriate force against those nations, organizations, or persons he determines planned, authorized, committed, or aided the terrorist attacks that occurred on September 11, 2001."

However, the second part of that section would prove to be the driving force for what would amount to a near constant and enduring presence in the Middle East, which continues to this day: "or harbored such organizations or persons, in order to prevent any future acts of international terrorism against the United States by such nations, organizations or persons."

The phrase of the day was "Global War on Terror." The idea was that wherever terrorism was, the United States would be there, to hunt, capture, or kill those engaged in these politically motivated crimes. The terminology gave the president the latitude to expand and control operations as needed or, as cynics would say, essentially built in "mission creep."

Just prior to the AUMF signing, and in a dramatic show of support, the North Atlantic Treaty Organization (NATO) invoked Article V of the NATO charter for the first time in history. Known as the "collective defense" mandate, it decrees that an attack on one member state is an attack on all. Then, on October 2, the NATO Secretary General pledged the full support of NATO members to the United States in this new era of warfare.

In the days and weeks after 9/11, the stories of heroism began to be told. From Todd Beamer and those heroic passengers on Flight 93, to New York Fire Department (FDNY) Chaplain Mychal Judge who was the first confirmed fatality of 9/11, to the hundreds and thousands of harrowing, horrifying, and heroic stories of people simply helping people. But there was one story that I read about that for some reason stuck in my mind.

Welles Crowther was a twenty-four-year-old Boston College graduate, a financial trader, and a volunteer firefighter who donned a red bandana over his face and raced up and down the South Tower to help move friends, coworkers, and strangers to safety. For some reason when I heard about the story of the red bandana, and the anonymity of who that selfless person was running up and down the stairs with little regard for their own safety, it was something that really resonated with me. Maybe it was my idealistic love for heroic tales, or the desperate need for something good to believe in, but the "man in the red bandana" was a symbol of sorts to me that even in extraordinary circumstances, ordinary people can and should make a difference.

As Ground Zero continued to smolder, there was a bright sign that signaled that life was getting back to normal—a new normal: Saturday Night Live (SNL) was set to return. Reese Witherspoon was announced as the host with musical guest Paul Simon. I always loved SNL, so seeing the comedic genius from the cast was hopefully going to be not only a reprieve from the grief, but a sustainable prescription to move on. And while the cast had some great skits and segments, and Paul Simon's rendition of "The Boxer" was hauntingly beautiful, it was NYC Mayor Rudy Giuliani who really stole the show.

After 9/11, America had grown to love Rudy, and he rightfully earned the accolade of "America's Mayor." He showed courage and conviction on the global stage and even served as a rallying point of sorts for every American living in a state of uncertainty and fear. And as if America couldn't love him more, he then delivered one of the best one-liners in the history of SNL. Executive producer Lorne Michaels, standing next to the mayor, who was flanked by members of the New York Police Department (NYPD), FDNY, and the New York Port Authority, asks him, "Can we be funny?" And the mayor, with his thick New York accent and lateral lisp responded with perfect comedic timing, "Why start now?"

Seemingly with that, American flags began being raised again to full mast. Ribbons and patches honoring first responders adorned athletic uniforms, nearly everywhere you looked was a FDNY or NYPD shirt, and "United We Stand" bumper stickers were plastered on every surface imaginable. America was indeed united, and our collective response to one of the darkest days in our history made this young American deeply proud of my country and even prouder of my countrymen.

One moment that still gives me chills was Game 3 of the World Series that year. As if scripted in Hollywood, the New York Yankees—who, like them or not, are a global symbol of America—were set to face the Arizona Diamondbacks. The series took place only seven weeks after the attacks, and as the away team, the first game back at Yankee Stadium was planned for Game 3—less than ten miles away from Ground Zero.

Major League Baseball asked President Bush to throw out the first pitch, and due to security concerns and ongoing threat streams, he was advised to throw out the pitch for Game 1 of the series. But there was a problem, the game was in Arizona, and Bush knew there was only one place he could do it—from the mound at historic Yankee Stadium.

Sixty feet, six inches. That's the distance from the pitcher's mound to the back of home plate. Generally, people throwing out a first pitch do so from somewhere in between the mound and home plate to stave off the chances of an errant throw or, worse, not having enough power and strength to get the ball all the way to and over home plate. And if throwing a first pitch in front of the world wasn't tough enough, the president would have to do this while wearing a bulletproof vest underneath his jacket.

Warming up in the stadium's batting cage, President Bush—fully aware of the importance of this moment—was photographed by numerous outlets looking like a professional athlete, focused on the task and the mission at hand. President Bush, a former Yale baseball player himself and part owner of the Texas Rangers, then received some succinct and sage advice from the Yankee's future

Hall of Fame shortstop Derek Jeter: "Don't bounce it, they'll boo ya."

Legendary Yankee announcer Bob Shepherd introduced the president, and an incredible roar came from the crowd as Bush defiantly walked to the mound. Wearing an FDNY jacket, he gave a thumbs up to the crowd and then delivered one of the most important pitches in the history of America's pastime. A perfect strike. Who says baseball isn't romantic?

Back home, my sophomore high school football season was coming to an end and the winter soccer was picking up. As a dual sport athlete there was always something extracurricular going on. But while a lot of my teammates were busy planning their summer camp tours, talking to college scouts, and sending out recruiting tapes, in my mind, I had already made the decision that I would serve. I grew up reading the adventurous tales of Jack Ryan in the Tom Clancy novels, watching Steven Seagal take over an entire battleship with a chef's knife, and seeing Chuck Norris defeat violent terrorist organizations armed with a rocket-firing motorcycle. I also wanted to be one of the guys with a patch on his shoulder. And my desire to serve was solidified in the aftermath of 9/11. And if that wasn't compelling enough, the lengthy history of my family's service weighed just as heavy.

My grandfather Anthony "Tony" DeMarco passed away when my dad was ten years old. Tony was the son of Italian immigrants—Francesco and Theresa—my great grandparents, who arrived in the United States in 1907 through Ellis Island aboard the SS *Europa*. The manifest that we found from the ship showed that they arrived in this country with little more than a pocket full of change and dreams of the new world. Grandpa Tony would go on to serve in the United States Army from 1938 to 1946. After the war, Tony married a local girl, June Jeanine Lohrig, and started their life with their child, Frank DeMarco: my dad.

After Grandpa Tony's passing, my grandmother and father moved to Alexandria, Virginia, and she began working at the Smithsonian Institute in Washington, DC, where she then ultimately met a man named "Woody." Woody was a navy veteran from Baltimore and was one of the key personnel moving vehicles, aircraft, and equipment into the new and highly anticipated National Air and Space Museum.

Charles Woodrow Wilson Lohrig, "Woody," or Grandpa Woody, was born November 11, 1918, Armistice Day, and joined the United States Navy in 1939. He then served aboard the USS *Houston*, based out of Pearl Harbor. The USS *Houston* was rumored to be the fastest ship in the Pacific Fleet and was also reportedly one of President Franklin D. Roosevelt's favorites; it took him on a twenty-four-day cruise in 1938. The *Houston* later became the flagship of the Asiatic Fleet.

On December 7, 1941, when the Empire of Japan attacked Pearl Harbor, the USS *Houston* was conducting maneuvers out in the Pacific. This meant two things for the "Galloping Ghost of the Java Coast": first, she was safe from the attack, and second, she was already forward deployed near the newly established front lines of the Pacific Theatre of War.

The *Houston* soon joined up with the short-lived American-British-Dutch-Australian Command (ABDA), a multinational force under one unified command. For the early part of 1942, she conducted joint maneuvers and patrols with ABDA and saw action in the Battle of Makassar Strait. On February 26, the *Houston* would be fully tested in what was the largest naval battle since the Battle of Jutland in World War I: the Battle of Java Sea. This battle would see several of the allied ships of ABDA Command sunk as HMS *Perth* and the USS *Houston* escaped to resupply.

On February 28, 1942, steaming together, the *Perth* and *Houston* encountered a Japanese destroyer. The *Perth* engaged the destroyer, however, just over the horizon was what seemed like nearly the entire Japanese fleet; they were surrounded. The *Perth* and *Houston* evaded the enemy for some time but were blocked by the overwhelming enemy fleet. Later that night, and into the morning of March 1, after valiantly fighting off an overwhelming force, both the *Perth* and *Houston* were sunk off the coast of Indonesia.

Of the 1,061 sailors and marines aboard the *Houston*, only 368 survived the battle. Those who survived and were able to swim to shore were then immediately taken as prisoners of war (POWs) by the Japanese. Details on what happened next are tough to find, but according to research conducted by the USS *Houston* Survivors' Association, Woody and his shipmates were then sent to Singapore and the Changi Jail POW Camp. There they were forced into slave labor, along with 17,000 other allied POWs, where they built the Burma-Thailand Railway, otherwise known as the "Death Railway," that inspired the movie *The Bridge on the River Kwai*, which many of the POWs from the *Houston* abhorred.

Woody and the survivors of the *Houston* were shipped to several different locations, where the stories of what they encountered, the conditions they lived in, and the treatment they received are horrific. Ultimately, they ended up in Iwate, Japan, a northern mining town along the west coast of the island. The story that I grew up hearing is that one day, the Japanese just abandoned their posts. The POWs were extremely suspicious that this was a trap, so they didn't leave the camp for fear that they would be murdered. And it wasn't until they saw US and allied planes overhead that they knew something had happened, and that just maybe their nightmare was over. And in April 1945, after forty-two months of slave labor, malnourished and subjected to near daily beatings and torture, the surviving 291 of his shipmates were liberated by US Forces.

I always knew Grandpa Woody was a hero, but I never really knew why, or what that really meant. He never talked about his service, and much of what we know now is from after-the-fact research that our family has done. But when he passed away because of Alzheimer's disease, he was buried with full military honors at Arlington National Cemetery. The twenty-one-gun salute, the playing of "Taps," and the presentation of a folded flag on behalf of a grateful nation still are burned into my memory. It was a solemn and beautiful ceremony on America's most hallowed ground.

Grandpa Holmes, my maternal grandfather, was a pistol. There's a saying about marines, "no better friend, no worse enemy," and Grandpa Holmes surely embodied that spirit. Hell, even his boat was named *Semper Fi*. He had initially joined the Army but then enlisted in the United States Marine Corps as the oft-forgotten Korean War kicked off in 1950.

Unfortunately, much less is known about Grandpa Holmes's service and his story except that he was awarded the Purple Heart. He never talked about his service but loved talking to others about theirs. He was also a gentleman's gentleman. The kind of man who made you feel like the center of the universe when he interacted with you, because he was in fact the center of the universe. He was revered and respected by all, and he showed that same respect to everyone he encountered. We would often visit Grandpa, and he would take me to the St. Petersburg Yacht Club. And, yes, while he was a paying member, the staff always went abnormally out of their way when "Bill" walked in. We'd have long dinners where he would quiz me on history and arithmetic, and then sharpshoot my chivalrous skills on how to order food for a date, how to properly pull out a chair, and how to signal to the waiter you're finished. And when I wasn't being interrogated, he would often bet me to try to eat a spoonful of hot horseradish or something else that would certainly turn my stomach upside down.

While Grandpa Holmes taught me a lot about, well, everything, I'd be remiss if I didn't mention how integral, tough, strong, and instrumental the women in my life were. With my paternal grandmother, Jeanine, my maternal grandma, "Nana," my mom, my mom's best friend and "second mom," Ms. Lauren, and countless others, I grew up lucky and incredibly fortunate to have such a loving and supportive family.

Chapter 3

STRAITS AND NARROWS

"Everyone has a plan until they get punched in the face."

This quote is attributed to former heavyweight boxing champion, Mike Tyson, and I can't think of a more applicable quote to life. Granted, Tyson was talking about his upcoming fight with Tyrell Biggs, but the essence of what he said reverberates across all aspects of our lives. We can have the best laid plans, put ourselves in the premier positions to attain our goals and reach our dreams—but this little thing called "life" always gets a say.

Looking back now, I can say with confidence that one of the most important lessons I've learned is that there are things in life that we simply are helpless to affect, impact, or do anything about. Frankly, there are far too many things that we simply don't have control over. But in saying that, and the essence of what I'm getting at is simply this: the only thing we can control is how we react to adversity. That right there is probably the single most important lesson that I've learned by going through adversity and crucibles both in my personal life and professional career. But, as a sixteen-year-old kid in Sarasota, Florida, dealing with adversity was the last thing on my long list of teenage priorities.

On a spring morning, I woke up to my mom coming into my

room, unceremoniously waking me up to tell me that she was moving out. And that movers were coming to pick up and pack my things shortly. And moreover, she was leaving my dad. My initial thoughts: "What the $@*% just happened?" I went to bed one night, a perfectly imperfect teenager in a standard middle-class household and woke up another $@*%ed-up statistic in a broken family. At sixteen years old, with all the standard growing pains and angst of teenage adolescence and now coupled with this, it was essentially, as acclaimed author Malcom Gladwell calls it, my tipping point: "the moment of critical mass, the threshold, the boiling point."

For all intents and purposes, I had a wonderful childhood, surrounded by loving parents and family. Were there issues among us? Of course. But I was always insulated away from any of the problems. My parents wanted to protect me as much as possible from the behind-the-scenes issues, the family drama, or the real-world problems that we all faced. To no fault of their own, they did what they thought was best for me. However, in reality, it emotionally handicapped me. The natural emotional resilience I would have learned, adapted, and inculcated was nonexistent. I was a physically tough kid, sure, but that was just superficial. The reality was that I had little to no emotional intelligence but enough false confidence or brashness to think that I could tough it out and never ask for help.

My parents' divorce is no fault of anyone—it is, as they say, "something that happens"—but to me it was the end of the world, and I blamed them both. My mom for making the decision to move out, and my dad for not being able to fix it. I spread out the disdain equally across all parties, and it wouldn't be until years later that I was able accept this new normal.

To say that I soon became the kid that parents warned their

children about is an understatement. Armed with a fake ID, a car, and a "zero $@*%s given" attitude, I was solely in the driver's seat of what was surely a road trip down the highway to demise. It's not very often that a kid, especially one with what you would have thought had so much promise, does a complete 180-degree turn in life. And if that does happen, odds are that there is some external influence or action that is driving it.

The adults around me, my coaches, teachers, parents of friends, nearly everyone, saw this change. It was hard to miss it. I began skipping school, talking back—and/or shit—to teachers, smoking cigarettes, drinking, getting into fights, and being basically the polar opposite of my previous self. "New Adam" was the antithesis of "Old Adam," as my actions weren't just out of character. I was a different person altogether.

And for the most part, everyone accepted it as who I was. I was no longer the smart, respectful, two-sport athlete with a bright future. Now, I was the truant degenerate with little regard for anyone or anything. Looking back, I see a lot of myself in some of the high school–aged players I've had the opportunity to coach and mentor in recent years. And it's now that I realize, in hindsight, that if only someone, a coach, a teacher, a family friend, anyone really, had asked me three little words, a simple in passing statement that we take for granted, I would have shattered into a million pieces: "Are you okay?"

The American Psychological Association (APA) defines trauma as "an emotional response to a terrible event." But when we think of trauma in modern parlance, we often think of catastrophic accidents, such as violence or combat. We don't often think of the everyday events that, while not leaving visible marks, cut to the core inside of us. For me, my parents' divorce was just that.

Although trauma can occur at any age, it has particularly

debilitating long-term effects on children's developing brains. Exposure to these experiences is often referred to as an Adverse Childhood Experience (ACE). ACEs, as the Center for Disease Control identifies them, "are potentially traumatic events that occur in childhood (0–17 years)." In their definition, they focus on physical events such as domestic and sexual abuse—truly abhorrent crimes—but acknowledge that ACEs can include "aspects of the child's environment that can undermine their sense of safety, stability, and bonding," like growing up around substance abuse problems, mental health issues, or instability.

Now I know what you're probably thinking. How in the hell can I equate the physical trauma of abuse with the emotional distress of a common parental divorce? But we must realize that during a child's formative years, anything that happens—whether it's getting hit with a baseball playing catch, being bullied at school, or being sexually abused by a trusted guardian—can have traumatic impacts on the formation of that child and the future physical and mental health adulthood. We've seen tremendous strides in addressing mental health concerns and destigmatizing mental health in recent years. But in the early 2000s, that simply wasn't the case.

Had anyone approached me with an empathetic manner instead of with a villainous accusatory viewpoint to try to see what was happening and asked me that, they would have seen a want-to-be-badass-teenager melt into an emotional train wreck. But it never happened. I was too far gone in their eyes.

Instead, I was written off, cast out, laughed at, and scolded. This all only perpetuated my anger and angst, driving me even further into the hole of despair that I continued to dig. The emotional numbness I felt grew into what felt like a detachment from society. No one understood me, and there was no one I could confide in.

Battles Within

There is no worse feeling than when people give up on you. It's like quicksand. The more you struggle and try to fight it, the quicker you get sucked into the abyss. One by one, you begin to shut down. You can see it happening right in front of your eyes. And as you slowly sink into the pit, you realize that you are helpless. There's no rescue crew coming, no rope or ladder, no hand up and out, and then you realize that everyone who could have helped has abandoned you. And there is nothing you can do about it.

Chapter 4

DARING GREATLY

There's a quote in the 1994 hit movie *Rudy*—the story about a broke, five-foot-nothing kid who goes from working in a factory to getting accepted to the University of Notre Dame and earning a spot on the Fighting Irish football team—that is one that will forever resonate in my life. The scene is that Rudy is having lunch with his best friend, Pete, after a shift at the mill. It's Rudy's twenty-second birthday, and Pete hands over a paper bag to Rudy, and in it is a vintage Notre Dame varsity jacket. Rudy then puts it on and asks Pete, "How does it look?" To which Pete responds, "You were born to wear that jacket."

As Pete lights up a cigarette, Rudy tells him, "You're the only one who ever took me seriously, Pete." With his cigarette hanging out of his mouth, Pete responds, "Having dreams is what makes life tolerable."

Now I don't know if that happened in real life, or if that story is all that factual. But I always secretly wished there had been that lightning strike–like event that occurred for me, or some inspirational message I received that made me get up off my back and back on the straight and narrow road. And trust me, I was always looking for one. I also hoped that one day I'd have some romantic dare-to-be-great moment that would change my life and my small little world: the rescue lifeline for a lost and scared kid.

But the truth is—and something that I've found out much later—those moments happen every day. We are just sometimes blinded to them by ambition, distractions, or worse, failure to act on them. Because too often in life we wait for some sign or external indicator to do what we know we should have been doing in the first place. It was time for me to stop $@*%ing around and get my shit together.

But that's easier said than done, especially as a now seventeen-year-old kid. My junior year in high school was the time when everyone became laser focused on their collegiate future, where they were going to go, what they were going to study, and what high-paying job they were aiming for. As for me? Well, I was just trying to scrape by and graduate on time, and hopefully, the rest would figure itself out. I mean, I made the unofficial decision to join the military already, so I'd probably just ride that out. One problem, though. I'd still need to graduate.

I was never good at school. I always loved learning, loved exploring, but hated the structured aspect of it. I wanted to learn what I was interested in. Which meant algebra, geometry, biology, chemistry, and basically every other class took a back seat to what I was interested in: history, civics, and government. That disdain for the structured aspect of our education system coupled with my overall disregard for authority didn't help my cause academically. While I could ace any test and write college-level papers about the root causes of the American Civil War or the genesis of the United States Constitution, the other subjects, well, they just didn't matter to me. As a result, my report cards read like a Christmas tree: one or two "As" at the top and a preponderance of "Cs" and "Ds" at the bottom. It was required to have a 2.0 grade point average (GPA) in order to graduate in the State of Florida, and by the middle of my junior year, I was hovering a bit south of that number. The door was closing fast, and I was $@*%ed.

From a football perspective, it was around this same time that I went from being a defensive position player—still a scrawny kid whose false bravado was much bigger than his brain—with the additional task of being a kicker, to focusing solely on placekicking. I wasn't the biggest guy, or the fastest, but with my soccer background, I figured that kicking a ball through uprights couldn't be that hard. And quite frankly, I got pretty good at it. Good enough to start getting letters in the mail from several small colleges and universities about potentially playing college football. This was kind of strange because, for one, I was a better soccer player, and two, I wasn't even sure I was going to graduate high school!

College was nowhere near my informal five-year plan. I figured, if I could pull this thing out and squeeze by to graduate on time, then I'd just enlist in the military—like my grandfathers had—and then figure it out from there. This wasn't a bad plan, given the events of 9/11, and with now two wars going on at the same time—Operation Enduring Freedom and Operation Iraqi Freedom—it'd be one hell of an adventure. And hopefully, if it all worked out, I could then figure out how to get one of those rocket-launching motorcycles that Chuck Norris drove.

It was in a passing conversation with Coach John Sprague, our head football coach for the Riverview High School Rams, during an off-season football workout—I think I was wearing a navy shirt—that he asked me if I was going to join the navy. I told him I was thinking about it but wasn't too sure. Coach Sprague just kind of looked at me with a quizzical and puzzled look, as he chewed his unlit cigar. The kind of look where it feels like the person is seeing through your soul. Coach Sprague was a stereotypical football coach, the kind who can just look at you and without even saying a word will have you feeling exposed and vulnerable. Coach then said, in his hoarse and raspy voice, that he would introduce me to someone. Not that he wanted to, but he would.

Mr. Joe Urschel was a short old man who always hung around practice, even in the off-season. Always wearing a tucked-in polo, boat shoes with socks, and a baseball hat with the word "ARMY" in big block letters, Joe was at nearly every practice and workout we had at Riverview High School. Truthfully, I had no idea who he was, and even more candidly, I really didn't care. I was too self-absorbed then to really notice anything outside of my direct orbit.

My first few interactions with Joe were mainly about me learning about him. He had been an Air Force veteran and test pilot after graduating from the United States Military Academy at West Point in 1952. After the Korean War, he then got into the private sector and was active in numerous organizations that supported youth initiatives. I learned to respect Joe a lot, not only because he was a veteran, but because he took the time to speak with me. One interesting note with Joe was that he never really asked about things in my past. Everything that we talked about was forward-leaning or future-focused. He didn't concern himself with as much of who I was, but rather who I wanted to be. His willingness to take an interest in me goes to show that sometimes the littlest things can make the biggest difference.

I talked to Joe a lot, about my life, my goals, and my dreams. What I wanted to do, how I was going to do it, and what I needed to get there. Then one day, when we were talking at practice, he asked me, "So why not Army?"

I didn't really have a response. In hindsight, it's interesting that he didn't ask me, "Why not the army?" But he asked me, "Why not Army?" Two very different distinctions. I mean I certainly didn't rule out joining the Army, but I just wasn't sure exactly which direction I was going to go. I came from a navy family, with the Marine Corps falling under the Department of Navy— "the men's department"—and I just didn't have any experience with the Army. So, I explained in a rambling and roundabout way that I wasn't opposed to anything. And that I was just looking to serve, in any capacity, and see what happens next.

Then, like clockwork, about a week after that seemingly small conversation, I got a postcard addressed to me from the Army football office, United States Military Academy at West Point, not the army, but Army. It was a simple postcard with the faces of Presidents Grant and Eisenhower and Generals MacArthur and Lee, with the words "At West Point, much of the history we teach was made by those whom we taught."

I had heard of West Point before, but it always seemed like a mythical place. A place where the best and brightest from the elite tiers of American society go. It was the Ivy of the Ivies, a place that bred and forged past and future American leaders. Even saying the words "West Point" elicits a sense of secrecy and reverence that no other institution holds. Certainly not the place for a questionably below-average student from a public school with an even more questionable reputation.

I began to have conversations with some of the West Point coaching staff and quickly realized that the archetype of what I thought they wanted was in fact almost the complete opposite. From their viewpoint, and, yes, while grades mattered, the most important piece of prospective Cadets and football players was your reasoning for and desire to serve. I remember thinking to myself, "Wait, that's all? They just want to know that I want to be there? No way…"

Now in my senior year of high school, my dad and I took a trip up to West Point for a football game at the invitation of the team. To be fair, we also stopped by the Naval Academy and the Virginia Military Institute as well. But being at West Point in the fall football season is just something different altogether—which is why it is annually ranked as one of the best locations of college football. And from the second we entered the iconic Thayer Gate and stepped foot on the campus, I was sold. Not that they had to sell me on anything, as I was just thankful for the opportunity to even visit, let alone the very outside remote chance of attending.But it was that moment that I made a personal commitment to do anything and everything to join the "Long Gray Line." But then reality set in.

My grades were terrible, my standardized test scores were near the bottom, and I didn't have any political connections or capital to secure the required Congressional nomination to earn an appointment. For context, to get "in" to West Point, not only do you have to be qualified, but you also must be Congressionally appointed either through a local Congressional representative, a United States senator, the vice president, or the president of the United States. The errant ways of my previous couple of years made it nearly impossible for me to make up for the lost time.

Because the application process is long and lengthy, and there are numerous tasks along the way to complete, I made time to speak with one of my high school guidance counselors, Mrs. Bozarth, who ironically had two sons who were attending the United States Air Force Academy. Sitting in her office, she pulled up my grades and attendance records and almost burst out in laughter when I explained what my goal was. In the nicest way possible, she articulately tiptoed around the bottom line that there was no way in hell that I would get accepted nor even considered for an appointment.

But unfortunately for her, she had no idea that deep down, under the false façade that I had built as a defense mechanism, I was still the kid who was on the mound in a little league game after having just loaded the bases and looked at the coach in the eyes and told him that everything was all right—and proceeded to strike out the next two batters, leaving all runners on base without letting up one run. I was the kid who when the chips were down and our backs were up against the wall, always wanted the ball. And I was the same kid who when faced with people picking on someone would stand up and say, "Show me where they are, and I'll take care of them." And fortunately for me, I had nothing to lose.

I was on a mission. As Cameron Poe, played by Nicholas Cage, says in the 1997 hit movie *Con Air*, "It's not exactly Mai Tais and Yahtzee out here—but let's do it."

In between working two jobs as a camp counselor and a mall retail salesman and playing two varsity sports, I devised a plan that if I could get my grades high enough to graduate with something anywhere close to a 3.0 GPA and then get a really, really high SAT score, with a whole lot of luck and some divine intervention, I might be quasi-competitive. In hindsight, it was a fool's errand. At that point, I had maybe a 2.0 GPA, so it was mathematically impossible to rectify my errant academic choices and ways. My plan had all the hallmarks of an idealistic teenager who thinks he is impervious to the natural laws of common sense. But none of that mattered. I had my orders; it was time to move out.

I literally relearned every subject I could, from mathematics and chemistry to geometry and English. I took every College Board prep course I could find. Hell, my dad even enrolled me in night classes at a local college where he served as an adjunct professor. I was determined to make this new dream a reality and spent nearly every waking day of the summer going into my senior year to make it happen. I was Rudy.

Senior year, I was advised to not take the year off, like most seniors do. It was advice that I fully heeded; I had a lot of ground to make up, and with my lofty academic goal, it would mean I'd have a full schedule of tough courses—to not only salvage my GPA but demonstrate that I was serious. The degenerate in me was rather pissed at this new change in direction from the spiraling road to ruin to the straight and narrow. But while I had this new intrinsic motivation, not everyone was on board.

I had one teacher in particular who really despised me. She had a daughter who was in my grade, which probably added fuel to the fire of her consternation toward me, because I was the kid parents warned about: a badge that, I can retrospectively say, I probably did deserve.

For my classmates, early admission decisions began to be received in the fall of my senior year. And almost like how the leaves change from the seasons, the senior year high school wardrobe changed from Abercrombie and Fitch button-down shirts and Lacoste polos to university sweaters and college mascot shirts, a subtle flex for the superficial hallways. One day, in this one particular class with this one particular teacher, we all went around the room in a futile exercise where everyone announced which school they would be attending. One by one, my classmates proudly announced, "University of Florida," "Wake Forest," "Duke," "Florida State," and then it came to me. While my classmates had their futures secured, mine was still in doubt, in flux, and filled with uncertainty. "Well, I'm still waiting to hear back from West Point."

The silence was only cut by the smirk and muffled scoff of the well-to-do kids who were generational legacies at their soon to be alma maters. And if the reactions of my peers weren't enough to set me off, I remember this particular teacher giving me a look that had the expression of both disdain and condemnation. I'll never forget the feeling of inferiority among my peers, the humiliation I felt as the spotlight was on me for the wrong reason. The impostor syndrome that I felt was both cutting and palpable. I'll never forget that moment.

To quote William Earnest Henley, "I [was] the master of my fate." Undeterred, I continued my mission to not just prove to myself that I was good enough but foolishly to show everyone who doubted me that they bet on the wrong horse in this race— "Charlie Mike."

After months of preparation, I was scheduled to take the SAT for what would be the last time before my application was submitted. It was my third time taking the grueling hours-long test. But this time, I had prepared, and I was confident. I had spoken to several people associated with West Point, both graduates and admissions officers, and their guidance was essentially that, to pull this "Hail Mary" off, I'd need to score a minimum of a 1300 out of 1600 on the SAT score scale.

The newly found overachiever, I made my target score 1350. It was a lofty goal, but with all the hours spent "solving for x," practicing analogies, and deciphering wordy passages to glean the subject and intent of absolutely ridiculous written passages about ridiculous topics, it seemed reachable. The trashy magazines that I'd read while inventorying the latest trendy shirts at the mall were replaced with all the gimmicky study materials I could find in the clearance section of the local bookstore. I was determined and just knew that it was all going to pay off.

After weeks of preparing, my fate came down to a few hours

on an early Saturday morning. Waking up, eating breakfast, and heading to campus, I knew it was game day. I had the inspirational Rudy soundtrack playing on the drive in. Whether it was nerves, exhaustion, or compartmentalization of the crucible that is the SAT, I don't remember the test, but walking out of the classroom afterward, I felt confident in my performance. I prepared well, and therefore I should do well because that's how life works, right?

It was a couple of weeks before the score report came out. I would race home every day to check the mail to see if there was a thick envelope from the College Board. I was excited to see the score report but also didn't want my mom to see it and open it before me—on the off chance that it didn't go the way that I prayed it did. And then one day, it arrived.

It's not very often that your life hangs in the balance of a simple envelope, but for me it did. Because the contents of that letter not only determined my short-term future; for me it was more than that. It was my chance to prove to everyone who doubted, put off, and demeaned me that I was worthy. A notion that I since have realized was just as foolish and wasteful as some of my other quixotic ideas. I didn't waste any time on theatrics; I ripped the envelope apart until I found the score sheet. And staring back at me, with a sense of dramatic irony, in dark bold, were the numbers 560 and 490, for a total of 1050.

I didn't wallow, I didn't cry, and I didn't panic. I just let the feeling of failure sink in. The hopes and dreams that I had built up over the past year, on what was already a long shot opportunity, all came crashing down in one fell swoop. But it was what I deserved. I had waited until the eleventh hour to get my shit together, work hard, and try to make something out of the years I wasted away in a self-imposed pity party for my situation.

I contacted my recruiting coach, Coach John Mumford, to let him know the news. I understood what this meant and graciously thanked him for even the glimmer of hope that this opportunity presented. But what was interesting was that instead of hanging up, he stayed on the phone. Instead of writing me off, he talked about next steps. And instead of giving up on me, he simply said, "Well, Adam, have you ever heard of the Prep School?"

One thing I absolutely believe in is the concept of "providence," the idea that all things happen for a reason. Because if there's one thing I've learned, it's that coincidences happen far too often to be random. For instance, had I not veered off the straight and narrow because of my parents' divorce, had I not been an asshole teenager, had I not been wearing a navy T-shirt that led me to meet Joe Urschel, and had Coach Mumford given up on me, who knows what would have happened or where I would be.

But because all these things did happen, I was offered the opportunity to attend the United States Military Academy Preparatory School at Fort Monmouth, New Jersey. And contingent on my successful completion, I would then be appointed to the United States Military Academy at West Point, where I would play for the Army football team.

It's funny now, looking back. I had just the right combination of arrogance and ignorance to think that I could do what everyone else thought was nearly impossible. And while the path to my dream was a bit different from my peers and certainly didn't go as planned, the end state would be the same.

As for that teacher who despised me and my classmates who embarrassed me, when word got out that I signed a letter of intent to attend and play football at the United States Military Academy at West Point, through the prep school, of course—a small nuance—the local newspaper put my face on the front page of the sports section with the caption, "Ram's DeMarco will play for Army." And the day after the story ran in the *Herald Tribune*, I just happened to pick up a copy on my way to school and slip it underneath that teacher's classroom door. A move that this soon-to-be Cadet Candidate smiled at, and the former degenerate applauded.

Chapter 5

THE LONG GRAY LINE

About an hour's drive from New York City, high above the winding Hudson River sits a revolutionary era fortress named Fort Putnam. Built in 1778, Fort Putnam was one of several forts built to prevent British naval vessels from sailing upriver after the victory at Saratoga. The emplacement of these forts and batteries was ideal because, at this specific point, the Hudson had an *S* curve, which caused unfavorable winds, strong currents, and numerous fields of fire on enemy ships as they tried to traverse the windy Hudson River. George Washington called this area the "key to the continent." Its importance was such that along with the fortifications, the Continental Army emplaced a 550-meter (1200-feet) chain across the river to prevent the British from even attempting to pass: the Great Chain.

Over time, the location became vital to the Continental Army's success as Washington set up a headquarters just a few miles north along with a large encampment. Washington put famed General Benedict Arnold, renowned for his exploits in the Battle of Saratoga, in charge of the post. And it was here that Arnold would then go from hero to villain, as it was the fortifications at West Point that he tried to hand over to the British in a traitorous plot.

It's also here at West Point that, in 1802, President Thomas Jefferson established the first military academy to educate and train military officers to build, protect, and defend these newly United States. And over generations and centuries, these historic and hallowed grounds have produced some of the finest and most notable American military officers in the history of our country.

When I arrived at West Point in the summer of 2005, after spending a year at prep school down in New Jersey, I began what would be a forty-eight-month adventure that would test every bone, emotion, and ounce of my being. But first, I'd have to endure "Beast Barracks": the first summer as a "Plebe"—a freshman, in civilian parlance.

Beast Barracks is a nearly two-month crucible that was a mixture of Army Basic Training, college orientation, and indoctrination to the "Long Gray Line." We learned how to fire various weapon systems while memorizing West Point songs like the Army fight song "On Brave Old Army Team" and the traditional "Sons of Slum and Gravy" rally song, all the while getting ready to take on what is arguably one of the most rigorous academic course loads in America. For me, Beast Barracks was rather easy. And it's not because I'm some sort of athletic stud, or the most "squared away" Cadet, but because I can find humor in any situation. While other Cadets were nervously reciting General Schofield's famed "Definition of Discipline" or frantically trying to get a mirror-like shine on their shoes, I was often daydreaming of the beach, drawing cartoons, or imagining what my friends were doing at that exact moment at their "regular colleges."

The keys to surviving West Point are relatively simple: make it through your first year, keep a sense of humor, work together, and don't violate the Honor Code. The Honor Code at West Point is the single most important aspect of the Academy. For Graduates, it is one of the most sacred aspects of West Point. But for Cadets, it is by far the most fear-inducing aspect of Cadet life. The code is relatively simple: "A Cadet will not lie, cheat, steal, or tolerate those who do." The first three stipulations of the code are relatively easy, because those are actions that we—as individuals—have agency of and direct control over. However, it's that fourth clause that is the hardest.

The "Toleration Clause" essentially says that, as Cadets, we have not only a moral obligation but a codified duty that if we are witness to any violation of the Honor Code, we then must take the necessary steps to rectify the situation. What does that mean? It means that if our roommates, teammates, or best friends violate the Honor Code—whether it is lying to a superior, cheating on a test, or stealing something from another—we must turn them in, or become guilty ourselves of violating the Toleration Clause of the Honor Code.

For me, the Toleration Clause was frankly terrifying. I have always believed in being fiercely loyal to my friends and family. Would I be prepared to potentially turn in my friends if they violated the Honor Code in order to prevent myself from violating it? Doesn't that just turn me into a snitch, a narc, a backstabber? These were all ideas that I, along with nearly every Cadet, had thought of and wrestled with daily. But in retrospect, what I can say now is that the Honor Code is meant to not only teach and bestow the ideals of honorable living, but also to inculcate the idea of a higher loyalty.

As Cadets, our paramount loyalty wasn't to our friends, classmates, or teammates; it was to the institution of West Point. It was to the Long Gray Line of graduates who have come before us, and it was our responsibility to maintain the strength of the line through our adherence and commitment to the Honor Code. What is more, it is to prepare us to uphold our Oath of Office as commissioned officers in the United States Army.

As future Army officers, our oath of office would differ from the oaths of enlisted personnel. Whereas their oath states that they will "support and defend the Constitution of the United States," it also states that they "will obey the orders of the President of the United States and the orders of the officers appointed over (them)." The oath of commissioned officers, on the other hand, reads:

> "I . . . having been appointed an officer in the Army of the United States…do solemnly swear that I will support and defend the Constitution of the United States against all enemies, foreign and domestic, that I will bear true faith and allegiance to the same . . . and that I will well and faithfully discharge the duties of the office upon which I am about to enter." —*Oath of Office*, Department of the Army

These oaths, with histories dating back to the Revolutionary War, have a very simple difference that is sometimes glossed over, but it is one of the core responsibilities and tenets of officership. While enlisted personnel swear an oath to support and defend the Constitution, they also affirm to follow the legal orders of the officers they serve under. The West Point Honor Code is not merely designed to build and maintain an academy of the utmost ethical standards and conduct, but it is also to prepare future Army officers to make the hard and honorable choices in living up to, supporting, and defending the Constitution of the United States, and only the Constitution of the United States.

These aren't lessons that you can truly understand at the Academy, because most of your time is spent just trying to keep your head above water in managing the day-to-day tasks, class assignments, military demands, and general rigors of being a

Cadet. For me, these lessons would be crystalized later in life through what former Congressman John Lewis called "good trouble."

Along with churning out leaders of character for our Army, dedicated to a lifetime of selfless service, one of West Point's greatest unintended skills is identifying a person's weakness or fault. It's almost like everyone has a deep secret, and the Academy's inherent goal is to find it and exploit it. For instance, if you violate the Honor Code, and after going before an Honor Board—which serves as a jury—you aren't merely "guilty" of violating the Honor Code, but you are "found." You've been exposed.

Everywhere you turn at West Point, there's an underlying lesson to be learned. Whether it's delivering upper-class Cadets' laundry, being able to recite the meals for the day, cutting a cake into ten perfectly distributed slices, or briskly walking with your hands cupped and by your sides, there's a reason for everything at the Academy. For me, the most important lesson is written in plain sight, emblazoned on every logo, and carved into every building: the words "Duty, Honor, Country."

Father Edson Wood was the Brigade Chaplain at West Point, having been appointed to the position in 2003. He was a short, white-haired Catholic priest who had the innate ability to move crowds, masses, and audiences through his gift of oration. He had a flair in his speaking and absolutely mastered the art of the dramatic pause. His homilies and sermons almost always centered on the mission of West Point, which is to not only train America's next military leaders, but to instill in them a higher code of values to be leaders of character in this nation. His most famous refrain is one that still echoes in my life today: "'Duty, Honor, Country' is not a way of looking only at certain things, it is a certain way of looking at everything."

Because you simply don't just go to West Point, you live it. It's not just a college, it's an experience. And while in the end—if you make it—you'll raise your right hand to commission as a second lieutenant, it's not necessarily the destination but the journey that you must embody and embrace. And no one did that more than my friend Joel Namy.

Joel was a big awkward kid from Cazenovia, New York. An offensive lineman—and no offense to the fellowship of offensive line athletes—he wore thick glasses, had rosy cheeks, and was generally an all-around klutz; he was really a caricature in a lot of ways. Those factors, coupled with his massive frame and thick New York accent, and well, he wasn't hard to miss.

Joel and I quickly became friends during our Plebe year, mainly because we were each other's support network—two football players struggling to juggle the academic rigors of the nation's toughest service academy along with the requirements of playing college football. As plebes, Joel and I would often talk about what we wanted to do once we graduated—albeit we still had four years to go and innumerable hurdles and crucibles ahead—and what we thought lay ahead of us in the Army.

Joel would come to my room a lot during the first few months at the Academy. He was pretty good at chemistry, and I, well, the only attribute I offered was a bit of comic relief in an otherwise dreary gray prison. When we didn't have practice or a game, Joel and I would often spend Saturday nights watching the latest Paul Rudd romantic comedies and ordering take out from one of the nearby delivery joints. In between that we'd talk about the army, and Joel would tell me at length how he was going to graduate and become a Special Forces "Green Beret" and have a lengthy career in the army.

I can't remember exactly when, but during our Plebe year, Joel began to complain of back problems. He'd wince in pain getting up out of a chair in class, briskly walking through the hallways, and even standing still in formation. Over days and weeks, the pain went from a barely noticeable small hitch in his step to what became a noticeable limp, and finally to the point where he was walking nearly fully hunched over. He went to the athletic trainers time and time again, and each time they would give him an ice bag and tell him it was probably a muscle strain. But that just didn't seem right.

After several weeks of dealing with this pain, and by now resorting to having to roll himself down the hallways in a desk chair to get from one room to another, Joel was sent to get an MRI for his pain. Figuring it was rather routine, it didn't seem like a big deal to me, my classmates, or even my teammates at the time. I can't remember who told me, but later that day we found out the terrible news. Joel had cancer. The MRI revealed that his pain was caused by a cancerous tumor sitting on his sciatic nerve. In an instant, the hopes and dreams of a young kid becoming a Green Beret from Cazenovia, New York, were shattered.

Thankfully, it was operable, even after living with this for by now what amounted to a couple of months. Joel immediately left the Academy to undergo treatment, and many of us never had the opportunity to say goodbye. We packed up his things and put them in the basement storage rooms—knowing that the likelihood of him ever coming back to retrieve them was near zero. When we were packing his things up for storage, I came across one of his Battle Dress Uniform (BDU) jackets with his nametag sewn on to it. Granted, it wasn't my size, but I took the jacket, and for the remainder of my West Point career, I had it hanging in my football locker.

Playing football at West Point still ranks as one of my proudest achievements. It's America's most exclusive fraternity, a true brotherhood, that culminates every year with "America's Game," the Army-Navy game. Many of my best memories from West Point stem solely from the relationships and friendships I made on the football team and the random adventures we had. Whether it was the grueling morning workouts in the pitch-black cold of winter, the struggle of getting bused after spending days out on field exercises to run sprints in the middle of summer, sneaking off post to go drink with local college girls, or simply enduring the highs of victory and the lows of defeat, much of who I am I credit to Army football.

My junior year, Coach Gary Miller, a former high school coach from Georgia, took the reins as the Special Teams Coordinator. He was and is one of the greatest coaches I've ever played for or met, for that matter. He knew next to nothing about the mechanics of kicking but was the first person to watch the rest of our specialist crew—kickers, punters, and long snappers—to learn the art of putting a spiral on a football from punting it, how to get a near perfect and on target end over end field goal kick, or how to snap a football between your legs with laser-like precision. Yet, while he couldn't coach us specifically in our craft, that didn't mean he didn't hold us accountable.

Going into my now junior year—"cow year"—I was the presumptive starting kicker based on the class seniority I had, but I still had to compete to win the job. During one of our spring scrimmages, I got the nod to go attempt a relatively long field goal—around fifty yards.

However, instead of having the first team special teams—with the starting snapper and holder—it was the second team, and while I had practiced with them before, our timing wasn't as synchronized as it should have been. But that should have been no matter. As I walked off my three steps back, looking at my target high up between the goal posts, I then took my two steps to the side. I closed my eyes, took two deep breaths, and gave the nod. The holder, Jonathan Bulls, made the call—"blue, blue, set…"— signaling to Walton Gouldin to snap the ball. Out of the corner of my eye, I saw the snap, took my stutter step, and approached the ball. It was a perfect snap and a perfect hold. But as I made contact and followed through, I then picked up my head only to realize that I had shanked the kick. And this wasn't just a kick that missed the uprights; this kick was a line drive that nearly took out some of the bystanders watching from the end zone. It was the kind of kick that you see on bloopers over and over repeatedly.

The practice ended on that kick, and aside from my embarrassment, I wasn't just disappointed in myself, I was furious. Our head coach, Stan Brock—a famed NFL offensive lineman with hands like bear paws—shook his head and blew his whistle to signal to the team to rally on him for a post-practice speech where he then tried to salvage the practice with some words about how we must get better every day. That message was clearly aimed straight at the guy in the number four jersey—me. Not only did I let myself down, but with one errant kick, I lost the confidence of my coaches and teammates. And while that's bad enough, I then made the situation one hundred times worse.

After we broke the team huddle, Coach Miller pulled Bulls and Walt aside to ask what happened. I explained that my timing was off because it was a different snapper and holder and that the snap was too slow, or the hold wasn't perfect. The snap was on target and on time. The hold was perfect. It was bullshit. He knew it, Walt and Bulls knew it, and I knew it. I was essentially blaming others for my fault. Coach Miller took it in stride and told us to break down our huddle and go into the locker room. But something didn't sit well with him. As we broke down our huddle, he called me to the side individually. I could tell he was still pissed about the botched kick, but whatever, it was over. However, that wasn't what he wanted to talk about. Coach didn't yell, he didn't cuss, and he didn't berate me, but the message of the one-way conversation was crystal clear. And one that continues to stick with me to this very day.

In short, he told me that what I had just done was not only inexcusable as a football player but lacking the character of an Army football player and future Army officer. I had failed to take accountability of my mistake and instead blamed others for my failure. As a leader, he expected more, and he demanded more. Because while today it was just a field goal, in the very near future, as an officer responsible for the lives of America's sons and daughters, it could be more dire circumstances with much more severe consequences and lives on the line. And he was absolutely right. I never got to thank Coach Miller for that, as it is one of the most important and invaluable lessons that I ever learned.

Later that same year, I received some incredible news. My friend Joel not only beat cancer, but he was coming back to West Point. Word spread like wildfire, as no one had seen him since Plebe year and we had only sporadically kept in touch via phone calls and emails. When he came back, it was almost like a ticker-tape parade. The relatively awkward kid from Cazenovia had beaten cancer and was now back at the Academy to fulfill his dreams. But things had changed. The cancer had not only affected him physically, but the emotional toll it took had a damning effect. He had changed. The conversations we used to have and assortment of topics we'd cover now had a darker tinge to things— much more morbid, frankly—but who could blame him. He had just endured months of chemotherapy coupled with the uncertainty of cancer treatment. All I could do was listen.

One day I came back to my room and saw a little shot glass with the West Point crest on it. Granted, I did have a penchant for "cadet borrowing" items from the mess hall—a term used at West Point to long-term borrow items that may or may not get returned—but I definitely didn't take a shot glass because frankly they didn't have them in the mess hall, nor booze. Then the door burst open and Joel, with a smile as wide as the Hudson, came strolling in to let me know that he got it to thank me for the support that I gave him over the past few years. Truthfully, I didn't feel like I had done anything out of the ordinary, except try to be a good friend. But to Joel, that meant more to him than I could have imagined.

Life was seemingly back to normal for Joel. While he couldn't play football anymore, he was able to get involved in other activities at the Academy. He became a member of several extracurricular clubs aimed at military tactics and essentially dedicated his life to becoming the real-life Rambo. I would make fun of him for his "brutalness," and he would just lap it up. It was almost like he never left.

However, one day, Joel came down with a slight cold and went over to "sick call"—the military equivalent of urgent care. Although he was in remission from the cancer and things were all on the up and up, the fact is that he was still extremely vulnerable, and any illness could be life threatening. After some lab tests, his results confirmed the worst: his cancer had returned. Leukemia.

I never saw Joel again. He would go through various courses of treatment in upstate New York. I only spoke to him maybe once or twice during that time. Whereas the first time he left we would receive several sporadic updates on his condition, this time it was seemingly much more dire. Because Joel's immune system had been depleted due to the new treatments, any interaction with someone who had even the mildest cough could be fatal to him.

In the summer going into my senior year—"firstie year"—I was sitting in the barracks when I received the simple four-word email from one of my classmates: "Joel Namy passed away." My heart sank. The days following the news, his family had to do what no family should have to, and that is prepare for the funeral and burial of their child.

The Army football team organized several buses to go up to the memorial service. All the coaches and players who were at the Academy would be in attendance along with what seemed like the entire town of Cazenovia. I, along with several of our company mates, was asked by his father to be one of the pallbearers: a task I certainly never wanted but an honor I could not be prouder to have.

Joel was buried with full military honors at the West Point cemetery. In a beautiful ceremony that Joel would have loved, and I could almost picture him standing there with us, in his freshly pressed uniform and brightly shining shoes, with a crisp salute. I'd been to military funerals before, but never like this. As the West Point Pipe and Bugle Corps played "Amazing Grace," and the sole bugler played the most solemn twenty-four notes in music, "Taps," both chills went down my spine and tears down my face. This was the first time I buried a friend, but unfortunately it wouldn't be the last.

During my time at West Point, at the conclusion of meals, as the entire Corps of Cadets is seated in a giant four-thousand-person mess hall at once, we would hear announcements from the Cadet Adjutant. These announcements would include trivial things such as information about club meetings, congratulatory remarks for Cadets who did something remarkable, or scores from the previous day's sporting events. And while they were normally instantaneously dismissed, there was one type of announcement that we would hear that would stop everyone in their tracks. I can't remember the exact verbiage—I'm getting old—but in my recollections it went something like this:

> "The Department of the Army is sad to announce the death of (insert rank) _____ (insert name) _____, West Point Class of (insert year) _____. _____ was killed while conducting combat operations in Operation (insert campaign) _____ in (insert country) _____. Please join in a moment of silence for our fallen comrade."

These announcements became all too common in the fall of 2008 into the spring of 2009, and with our graduation date set for May 23, 2009, this was something that weighed heavily on all our minds. And as the names were read aloud, it seemed it was more often than not that the graduate who was KIA—killed in action—was a relatively recent graduate, who was just sitting in the very same mess hall as us a year or two ago. That is the reality of the profession of arms, our next endeavor. And while these stark realities would be rather grim to some and fear inducing to others, for the collective Corps of Cadets, it was a bit of a different sentiment.

Because during that time, the surge in Afghanistan was ongoing and Iraq was still essentially on fire. So while during the academic days we discussed our thesis papers and studies of military history and the fundamentals of ethical officership, at night, at our local campus bar—"the Firstie Club"—the discussions were almost always focused on what post we were getting assigned to, what unit we wanted to join, and how fast we would deploy to go "see the elephant"—an old military phrase used for seeing combat for the first time. We couldn't wait to get out of the Academy and into the army, the "real" army.

Graduation day came faster than expected, and the days leading up to it were a fast blur spent sending out announcements and invitations, getting fitted for my new uniforms— "real" army uniforms—and making sure I didn't fall off the straight and narrow by getting into any trouble during my last couple of months.

One side note, while I may sound like I was a saint during my time at the Academy, I certainly wasn't. I had my fair share of fun, and in turn paid my fair share of consequences, through the torturous ritual of "walking hours." This punishment means that on weekends, you would dress in full uniform, with your rifle or saber, and walk around, across, and all over the main courtyard for hours, to work off your punishment and learn your lesson. And, if you are fortunate enough to be bestowed the privilege of walking one hundred hours, you then earn the unofficial title of "Century Man" or "Century Woman." And as a "Century Man" myself, a badge I wear with humorous honor, walking hours prior to graduation was not something I wanted or could bear to do.

Graduation day at West Point is the culmination of a week's worth of events, parades, ceremonies, and toasts to the graduating class. It's a whirlwind of a week because not only do you have to entertain the crowds of parents and prepare to go from a cadet to a lieutenant, but you also have to pack up four years' worth of uniforms, books, and other assorted random items to leave. Because in true army fashion, once you graduate and are a new "butter bar"—a nickname for a second lieutenant—you're expected to "be brief and be gone."

The pageantry and traditions of the actual West Point graduation ceremony start in the morning at breakfast, with a nutritious meal of waffles and ice cream. Then the first class returns to their barracks to don their graduation uniform: full dress over white uniform, carrying sabers. The rest of the Corps of Cadets assembles and marches up to Michie Stadium, my second home for the past four years, for the annually televised event that features nearly every senior and key leader from the Department of Defense.

Nearly every American has at one point in time seen the photo of the iconic hat toss: the moment after the graduating class receives their diplomas and is dismissed. It's a moment that even thinking about now still gives me chills. So, when our First Captain—the highest-ranking cadet—announced, "Class of 2009…class dis… (insert dramatic pause) …missed," I threw my cap so high in the air I nearly threw my arm out. And as I turned to my classmates to hug and high-five them, I felt tears streaming down my face. Unabashedly and unashamed, because for me it was a realization of a dream come true. Granted, it wasn't easy, and certainly it was the road less traveled, but for a kid who wasn't supposed to make anything of himself and was chalked up to be just another statistic, it truly was the achievement of a lifetime. But also, in the midst of the emotions and the cheering, I thought of my grandfathers, and my dear friend Joel.

Grandpa Woody passed away from Alzheimer's disease over a decade earlier, but Grandpa Holmes passed away while I was a cadet. He was diagnosed with cancer when I first started at the Academy, a cancer that we have since learned was almost certainly caused by the toxic water at Camp Lejeune Marine Corps Base. He would have been so proud of me.

When he was first diagnosed with cancer, a couple of my friends and I went back to Florida for spring break. But before heading down to our annual stomping grounds of Key West, I asked them to visit my grandpa in St. Petersburg and to bring their uniforms. He wanted to take us to dinner at the St. Petersburg Yacht Club, where he was the Commodore of the Power Squadron. My friends begrudgingly agreed, as we were hellbent on not being freshly shaven or even thinking about wearing a uniform. But that night, eating prime rib in our dress uniforms, listening to my grandpa's stories about life, love, and the Marine Corps, was a night I will never forget. And while I might be biased in saying this, it was one of his proudest moments.

I think it's only fitting then, as I stood on the field taking everything in on graduation day, present in a moment of pure jubilation, that I watched the hundreds of kids break through the chained barrier to go get a graduate's cap. While the graduation ceremony itself is extremely well scripted and orderly, after the cap toss, it quickly becomes anarchy as all the kids in attendance are allowed to run onto the field and get a cap. Their motivation isn't just because the caps are a cool souvenir, but because traditionally each graduate writes a little note in the cap and, more importantly, puts a couple bucks in there as well.

So, the night before graduation, after drinking my fair share at the Firstie Club and stumbling back to my room, I pulled out a couple bucks from my wallet, scribbled a small note on a torn piece of paper, and tucked it into my cap for some kid the next morning. Fully knowing that the message would probably be discarded immediately in favor of the last few bucks I had in my wallet. But maybe, just maybe, whoever grabbed that hat might read it, keep it, and later be inspired to follow it. My handwritten note was clear, concise, capitalized, and direct:

"AIM HIGH AND NEVER QUIT."

Chapter 6

ROADS TO WARS

D riving down a highway in the easternmost part of the Jordan along the borders of Iraq and Syria, staring out into the abyss of the barren desert, I thought it's hard to imagine surviving let alone living in this environment. The daily temperature shifts from scalding hot to freezing cold, and couple that with scarce natural resources, and it's a wonder why over millennia people settled here. But for all the difficulties that this environment would pose, there's a simplistic beauty to it.

I've always had an affinity for the Middle East, probably stemming from a childhood spent binge-watching Harrison Ford's adventures as Indiana Jones: finding treasures, punching Nazis, and saving the day. Granted, I had no experience in or with Middle Eastern culture, never met anyone from that region, and certainly never visited, but even as a kid, I was rather enamored by it. I wish I could say it's because as a child I had such an inquisitive and curious mind about the world around us, but in reality, it's because *The Last Crusade*, the third and best of the Indiana Jones series, was my favorite movie. But maybe wanting to be "Indy"—the fedora-wearing, whip-cracking, treasure-hunting hero—set me on this course that would ultimately find me sitting in the backseat of an armored Ford Expedition, armed with an old Nokia cell phone, a couple of energy drinks, a pack of cigarettes, and a tin of

Copenhagen. When I think back to this time, I often hear the hit song "Once in a Lifetime" from the Talking Heads:

"And you may find yourself in another part of the world . . .
And you may ask yourself, 'Well, how did I get here?'"

Graduating from West Point, a newly commissioned officer, wasn't the culmination of an adventure, but really the beginning. A beginning that found me spending the first couple of months of my army career traversing the United States, attending various mandatory schools, getting to spend some "quality time" at Fort Benning, and even having a stint back at West Point. But the highlight of sorts was my time at Fort Sill.

Located about an hour and a half southwest of Oklahoma City, Fort Sill is the mainstay of the small city of Lawton. And while most Americans have never heard of Lawton or Fort Sill, to anyone who has graced those red dirt roads, survived the barren summer heat, or had a penny beer at the famed Scooter's Country Bar, in many ways it's impossible to forget, although it's seemingly the land that time forgot.

Fort Sill was established as a military post in 1869. Originally, it was one of several outposts on the frontier during the campaign of General Philip T. Sheridan. While not a strategically important location, it became the main hub for logistics and supplies on the frontier. Fort Sill also has its fair share of history and association with notable figures in history. From General William Tecumseh Sherman—who was nearly assassinated at his own headquarters— to "Buffalo Bill" Cody, "Wild Bill" Hickok, and Henry O. Flipper, the first African American graduate of West Point. But the most famous, or infamous, individual associated with Fort Sill is the Apache medicine man and leader named Geronimo.

The stories of Geronimo's exploits are the stuff of legends, but one of the more controversial and conspiratorial legends associated with Geronimo has little to do with him, and more to do with Senator Prescott Bush, the father of President George H. W. Bush and grandfather to President George W. Bush.

In 1917, as the United States entered World War I, and having just finished his studies at Yale, Prescott Bush was sent to Fort Sill for training before being shipped out. The legend of what happened is highly contested, and while originally thought of as an "old wives' tale," it later became the subject of several lawsuits and is still an unsolved mystery.

The story goes that one night before shipping out to fight with the American Expeditionary Forces (AEF) in the trenches of Europe, Bush and several of his fellow fraternity brothers from Yale snuck out to the Apache cemetery on Fort Sill, dug up Geronimo's skull, and sent it back to his fraternity, which is also reportedly a not-so-secret society called "Skull and Bones."

I first learned about this legend as a Cadet at West Point, when I was sent to Fort Sill for Cadet Troop Leader Training (CTLT), which is an internship of sorts where Cadets go and serve in a unit and observe how the army operates. As football players, back in those days, nearly the entire team would go do this summer assignment—a rite of passage—together. Fort Sill, the home of the Field Artillery, was in many ways the second home for Army football; there was also a running joke that "FA," the abbreviation for Field Artillery, actually stood for "Football Alum."

Then the second time I found myself at Fort Sill was upon graduation from West Point. I was ordered back to Fort Sill to undergo the Officer Basic Course (OBC), which was a rigorous six-month course that trains and prepares newly commissioned officers to become Field Artillery Officers. Let me just say this, West Point was hard, yes, but OBC absolutely sucked. Sitting in class all day to learn about the physics of projectile motion and calculating these trajectories using antiquated wooden slide rules was hardly how I thought I would spend my time as a new army officer. And this certainly wasn't the life of a lieutenant that was depicted in *Top Gun*. And moreover, it was damn hard. The coursework, the homework, and being treated like shit from the leadership at OBC were enough to begin to plant the seeds of disdain in any new army second lieutenant. After several grueling months that certainly had more lows than highs, I arrived at my first "real" assignment and checked in to my unit at Fort Hood, Texas.

Located about seventy miles north of Austin, Fort Hood is home of the 1st Cavalry Division and one of the largest military installations in the entire Department of Defense, both in terms of personnel and land. Before arriving—or should I say gleefully leaving Fort Sill—I had worked out a deal with one of my roommates to trade assignments with him. He had a serious girlfriend, or maybe she was his fiancé—I can't remember—but he was slated to join the 4th Brigade, which was getting ready for an overseas deployment. I was slotted for 3rd Brigade, which had just come back. Given that he wanted to spend time with his significant other, and I, having spent the last four years at West Point hearing heroic tales of my recently graduated West Pointers, wanted to get into the action as soon as possible, with a couple of phone calls, we were able to work out this relatively easy switch. I had just signed myself up for my first combat tour in Iraq.

In March 2010, I signed into my first unit: the 2nd Battalion, 12th Cavalry Regiment, affectionately known as "Thunderhorse." When I first arrived, it was rather anticlimactic. In my mind, and through the expectations I built through the institutionalization from my days at West Point, I thought that I would come into my new unit, be handed a platoon, and be told to go take a hill then find, fix, and destroy the enemy. Boy was I wrong.

At West Point, lieutenant colonels are a dime a dozen, and familiarity with them begins to breed a sense of relaxed decorum and, although rarely, sometimes borderline contempt. The Army is not like that. In the Army, a lieutenant colonel, especially a battalion commander, the "Old Man," is the king of his kingdom. Battalion command is probably one of the most coveted positions in the Army because not only do you have the command responsibility, but you also have a level of autonomy under the Army's principle of "Mission Command": a Prussian-derived military strategy dating back to the Napoleonic Wars that promotes initiative, mutual trust, and decentralized decision-making. It's basically a way to empower lower levels to either take the initiative in something good, or to hold them accountable for something bad. So, when the boss wanted to see me, the new "LT," it was either going to be good, or really bad. And with my luck, the latter was much more probable.

Lieutenant Colonel Joe Holland, the son of a career Army officer, was not an imposing figure. But what he lacked in physical stature he surely made up for in intellect, judgment, and an impressively stoic demeanor. When I first sat down with the boss, I had already been working in the battalion for several months and was getting rather familiar with the organization and who the key leaders were— or more specifically, who hated me and who didn't. As I was doing the work of a lowly staff officer, my biggest concerns were if we had the briefings complete for the next meeting or if I was going to meet my daily deadline for some random report. So, for the boss to want to see me individually, I was sure that I had messed something up. Especially as we were gearing up for several critical training events prior to our deployment.

Before any unit deploys to combat, they have a laundry list of mandatory training they must complete. This encompasses everything from individual training, such as individual rifle qualification, all the way up to battalion-level training exercises. And then, of course, a litany of online training covering everything from operational security to equal opportunity. To set the conditions for these trainings, units go to a Combat Training Center (CTC), a culminating exercise that is the last major training event before a unit deploys to combat.

Lieutenant Colonel Holland was one of the types of people who spoke softly, and only once. And if he wanted something, at some point, whether in an hour, a day, or a month, he was going to ask about it. So, as I walked into his office, pen and pad in hand, I was bracing for whatever shrapnel or sabot rounds I was about to take. But to my surprise, he wasn't concerned about the weapons ranges I was assigned to run, the course on Information Operations I missed, or the new battalion Facebook page I created—where I misspelled our mascot, "Thunderhorse," by making it "Thunder Horse." Instead, he wanted to talk about our upcoming mission in Kirkuk, Iraq.

Kirkuk is a multiethnic, oil-rich city in northwestern Iraq and has been in the middle of competing claims between the Kurdish, Turkmen, and Arabic peoples for decades. Kirkuk is also the recognized capital of Kurdistan, which is a semiautonomous region of northern Iraq that was formally established in the 1970s as part of a peace treaty with the Government of Iraq.

Iraq has a very contentious history dating back to the founding of the Hashemite Kingdom of Iraq in 1921. Hashemites, or the House of Hashem, trace their lineage back to the great-grandfather of the Islamic prophet Muhammad, and have ruled the holy city of Mecca since the tenth century. The Hashemites were instrumental in the Great Arab Revolt of 1916, which was orchestrated in concert with the British, to defeat the Ottoman Empire in World War I.

It was during the beginnings of the Arab Revolt—nearly a year before the United States entered World War I—that a young British officer was assigned to work with the Arabs and specifically partner with Faisal I bin Al-Hussein bin Ali Al-Hashemi, the third son of Hussein bin Ali—the leader of the Hashemites. The British officer in question would not only later help to defeat the Ottoman Empire but also would author one of the seminal works on Middle Eastern culture entitled *The Seven Pillars of Wisdom*. His name was Thomas Edward Lawrence.

Thomas Edward Lawrence was a young and ambitious British officer. Having attended Oxford, Thomas Edward, or T. E., would then work as an archaeologist for the British Museum where he focused on Middle Eastern history and artifacts. At the onset of hostilities in 1914, T. E. Lawrence was on a map-making expedition exploring the Negev desert—the historical area of southern Israel in between modern-day Egypt and Jordan. The expedition was sponsored and funded by the Palestine Exploration Fund (PEF), an early British think tank that was the first organization dedicated solely to the study of the historical region of the Levant, or the modern Middle East. However, because of his knowledge, and the strategic importance of the Negev region, T. E. Lawrence's affiliation with the PEF became a cover, as the information he was gaining was now going to British intelligence in service of the larger war effort.

As part of his duties, T. E. Lawrence would also help identify key leaders, build capabilities, and oversee operations of the newly established Arab Army. In execution of these duties, he built a tight bond with Faisal, whom he nominated to lead the military operations, and together they orchestrated and conducted numerous insurgent campaigns against the Ottoman Empire from 1916 until 1918.

However, in 1916, Britain entered a secret treaty with France and Russia that would divide up and partition the Middle East once the Ottoman Empire was destroyed. In 1917, Vladimir Lenin came to power in Russia during the Bolshevik Revolution, and he came across a copy of the secret agreement. As Russia began to withdraw from the war, Lenin had his trusted agent Leon Trotsky publish the agreement in the *Izvestia* newspaper.

News of this secret treaty traveled quickly, and having learned about it for the first time, Lawrence felt that he had betrayed the Arab Army. Everything that he had worked for and sacrificed seemed all for naught. The agreement, negotiated by a Briton, Mark Sykes, and a Frenchman, Francois Picot, became known as the Sykes-Picot Agreement. Over a century later, much of the Arab world still resents the Western powers for their meddling in the geographic boundaries of this historic and religiously important region.

I hadn't heard of Kirkuk and frankly wasn't very familiar with Iraq. I vaguely remember Operation Desert Storm as a child, but I remember very clearly the beginnings of Operation Iraq Freedom. When the invasion began in March 2003, I, along with most Americans, was told and believed that this was an extension of the Global War on Terrorism. And while the politics of the war, from the search for Weapons of Mass Destruction (WMDs) to the initial invasion to the "Mission Accomplished" flight aboard the USS *Abraham Lincoln*, are all rightfully subject to intense scrutiny, none of that mattered to me. For me, personally, I was just ready to get into the action. Many of my friends had already been there—some multiple times—so when my opportunity came,

I couldn't wait to get over there.

So, with that ignorant eagerness, meeting with the boss had two end states that were diametrically opposed. The first was that I would be moved to a platoon leader position where I'd lead twenty soldiers in combat: every second lieutenant's dream. Or the second, and least desired, outcome, that I would be forced to stay back and conduct administrative tasks in the "rear detachment" while everyone else went forward to combat.

I left the meeting with the boss and went back to my little office, which was nothing more than a storage closet, an ethernet connection, and a foldable chair, wondering if I had just destroyed my career. I had briefly prepared for the meeting, did a couple of cursory searches about Kirkuk, enough to know that the city claims to be home to the Tomb of Daniel—the Biblical figure who survived being sent into a lion's den—but that was pretty much it. And given my general affable personality and what can be construed as abrasive tone of voice, coupled with the boss' stoic demeanor, I was nearly positive that none of my jokes landed and my attempts at small talk only further buried my chances of deploying.

Then as I got back into my daily grind of presentation building, one of my many bosses came by and remarked, "Hey, DeMarco, the commander is making you his KLE guy. Here's his upcoming schedule…"

My external response was, "Roger, sir. On it…" And I was handed a very neat and organized daily calendar with color-coded meetings, littered with small notes, and absolutely zero white space. But internally, I sarcastically wondered, "What the $@*% is a KLE!?"

Chapter 7

WELCOME TO IRAQ

L anding a C-130 Hercules in a combat zone is no easy feat—
so I assume. With a normal cruising altitude of around
20,000 feet, and cruising speed of over 300 miles per hour,
landing this over 150,000-pound cargo plane is both a science and
an art. Not only does the pilot have to bring this massive plane
to a stop on a shorter than normal runway, but they also must
contend with the imminent threats posed by a hostile enemy, such
as small arms fire (SAF), surface-to-air missiles, and air detonated
"improvised explosive devices" (IEDs)—yes, at one point that was
a thing. So, to mitigate these threats, pilots conduct what is called
an assault landing, or a "corkscrew" landing.

It's a rather standard maneuver where the pilot positions the
aircraft high over the runway and then rapidly spirals downward to
the ground and at the last second pulls up, touches down, and then
immediately reverses thrust to come to a quick and abrupt halt.
I've certainly oversimplified the impressive tactic, but one thing
I can't overstate is the absolute nightmare this is for the soldiers
in the back of the plane. Sitting face to face, in full kit, as you
spiral down to the ground, conventional wisdom would suggest
your concerns are focused on the threats—SAF, IEDs, etc.—but
in reality, your only thoughts are "I hope the soldier across from
me doesn't throw up."

When I got off the plane, head still spinning, I was immediately hit in the face with what can only be described as having a blow dryer six inches away from your face on full blast. Walking off the dark flight line, I began to get my bearings. In one of the tents, I see a clock. It's midnight, and it feels like it's 130 degrees. Then I see a massive steel-reinforced concrete blast wall, called a "T-Wall," with a rather impressive graffiti-style mural that says, "Welcome to FOB Warrior."

Forward Operating Base (FOB) Warrior, FOB Warrior, was an old Iraqi Army airfield located on the western side of Kirkuk. On March 23, 2003, as the initial invasion of Iraq was underway, the 173rd Airborne Brigade conducted the first large-scale airborne operation in over a decade when they jumped into Kirkuk to secure Bashur Airfield in what was called Operation Northern Delay. The airfield was used by the Iraqi Army during the Iraq-Iran war but had largely been deserted since then. However, by August 2010, when I first arrived, it was a bustling "metropolis" of an FOB. A city within a city. Hell, there was even a "mayor"—yes, the military calls the small organization in charge of the management of a base the "Mayor's Cell."

Keeping in mind that it was my first deployment, I was actually quite surprised at the amenities. For instance, there were two gyms, a coffee shop, several restaurants, a post exchange, and even a mini mall of sorts. In fact, it's an understatement to say that I was surprised. It was a far cry from what I had envisioned from the movies.

I arrived in Kirkuk on the advance party from my unit with the task of ensuring a smooth transition for the commander in the area of operations (AO). Before arriving, while in transit in Kuwait, we learned that the original mission set we had was changing and that our battalion would be essentially turning every platoon into a maneuver platoon—this meant that whether you were an infantryman or a line cook, you were going "outside the wire" on patrols. This caused an immediate reshuffling of units, which made our arrival in theater even more stressful.

As I was getting adjusted to the living conditions, I met the outgoing "KLE guy." He was a tall captain, several years older than me, meanwhile I was a brand-new lieutenant. He was a nice guy, but the fact that his position was being taken over by a brand-new lieutenant really didn't rub him the right way. He immediately knew that I was in over my head when I asked him, "So what exactly is a KLE?" To be fair, nowhere in my forty-eight months at West Point or seven months at my OBC did I ever hear or learn the term. Upon my inquisition, the older captain understood this was going to be a long two-week transition.

Come to find out, a KLE is a "key leader engagement." It's probably one of the most important aspects of military operations and engagements that I had never heard of. In an area of the world where the currency of the day isn't valued in gold but in relationships, KLEs became a de facto supporting effort for all operations and a key "no fail" task. Because we were training, advising, and assisting Iraqi Security Forces (ISF), we had to have their buy-in to empower them to do what we needed them to do, for us, to help them secure their own country—a rather circular methodology on paper.

The outgoing unit from the 3rd Infantry Division had put a tremendous amount of effort and emphasis into their KLE strategy, developing essentially volumes of dossiers about each particular leader in Kirkuk, with notes and readouts from every meeting from nearly every subordinate US commander and leader. These notes included specific details on meetings with everyone from the Provincial Police Chief, Major General Jamal Tahir, to the

Commander of the 12ᵗʰ Iraqi Army, Major General Abdul Ameer, to every politician and civic leader in Kirkuk.

However, what I quickly learned was, while they had processes and procedures in place to manage, document, and disseminate this information, Kirkuk itself was a vastly complex place, as it was a city with multiple ethnic backgrounds all vying and jockeying for power as the country continued to try to sort out its domestic political troubles. And they all understood that the key to power in the city didn't necessarily come from the will of the people, but the favor of the US military.

The Government of Iraq (GoI) was established after the dissolution of Saddam Hussein's Ba'ath Party and the adoption of a new Iraqi Constitution in 2005. The GoI was built as an Islamic, democratic, parliamentary republic, but with the goal of having it be representative of the diversity of Iraq. The problem is, Iraq at its core is a tribal country, setting the conditions for extremely volatile domestic power competition.

After the fall of Saddam, the GoI, under the watchful eye of the United States, developed a sectarian power-sharing agreement that guaranteed parliamentarian representation based on population percentage. This quota system would ensure that all stakeholders—Shia Arabs, Sunni Arabs, Kurds, Turks, etc.—would have some say, albeit varying, in the new GoI. But the dynamic of these conflicts, deeply seeded in historical claims and lineages, isn't something a person can glean from simply reading a book or reviewing a white paper. And to many, the establishment of these quotas, which seemed to mirror our own domestic two-party system, exacerbated the already fragile agreements and themselves set the conditions for what everyone feared for the fragile GoI: civil war.

As the KLE coordinator, or "KLE guy" as I tended to downplay my position, my job was not only to facilitate and attend all the KLEs that our commander would engage in, but I was also responsible for all the prep work for them, including writing talking points, taking notes, debriefing, and then publishing reports. Granted that this position was far from the knuckle dragging that I thought I'd be doing as a West Point Cadet, and even further from the art and science of conducting artillery strikes as I had trained for at Fort Sill, I found the work intriguing.

I was for all intents and purposes essentially a pseudo warrior-diplomat. And while my peers were going out on missions for days at a time, I quickly found myself coordinating efforts with the Department of State, nongovernmental organizations, and other government agencies in our AO.

I understood the gravity and importance of my newfound role and, much to my own chagrin, embraced it. It wasn't ideal and certainly wasn't what I envisioned I'd be doing when I daydreamed about combat as a cadet at West Point, but it provided some interesting experiences to say the least. However, I also knew that, given my inexperience, I was constantly going to be in over my head and would need to rely on individuals that I had never worked with, trained with, or hell, even met before: interpreters.

Habeeb was a local guy, Arabic, and had been working with US Forces in Kirkuk for nearly a decade. He knew everyone in the city, and everyone knew him. The US Government makes a point to hire local nationals on a contractor basis to help run the facilities, and at a certain point, they realized that having them also work as interpreters was a value add. But that's not to say that it didn't have inherent risk for both US Forces and the interpreters themselves. While everyone within the ISF of Kirkuk knew Habeeb, there were still concerns that his identity would be divulged and subsequently his life threatened.

Then there was Mohammed, "Moe," a quiet, incredibly smart

Kurdish guy who loved the New York Yankees. Moe was also local, having grown up in Kirkuk, however, he was Kurdish. Having both an Arabic and Kurdish speaker was not only helpful with language barriers, but as we would find out, there were various cultural sensitivities involved as well. For instance, some of the leaders we would work with would not meet with members of different ethnicities, and if they did, they would be standoffish, and the engagement would be hamstrung and ultimately fruitless. These were the everyday concerns that we would have to plan and forecast for in our preparation for our near daily excursions outside the wire. But the most interesting linguist who was on our team was Isaac.

I met Isaac during our deployment training at the Joint Readiness Training Center (JRTC) in Fort Polk, Louisiana. Unlike Habeeb and Moe, Isaac was an Army soldier, serving as a linguist. We were the same age, and in working with him over the course of several weeks, I came to learn that Isaac was born in Baghdad and immigrated to the states a couple years ago. And while I was being an asshole teenager and occasionally going to high school, he was serving as an interpreter for US Forces in Iraq. He told me how he had learned English as a kid from watching the Arabic version of MTV, how his family members were all lawyers, and how when he turned eighteen, he came to the United States to become a citizen and join the United States Army. He wanted to serve, he believed in supporting the people and the country of Iraq, but to him, more importantly, he believed in the spirit of America and wanted to pursue the American dream himself.

Their guidance was instrumental in ensuring that we wouldn't have any "ugly American" moments in building rapport with the key leaders of the ISF. As I got settled into my position, and the rest of our battalion began arriving, Operation Iraqi Freedom was nothing like I expected. It was almost like a regular Monday–Friday, 9–5 job for most people on the base. Meetings were scheduled around lunch times or gym sessions. And it seemed that every weekend there was some sort of morale-boosting event, such as salsa dancing night, bingo, or the occasional concert featuring the likes of the 90s hit band Smashmouth. It was very strange and sometimes surreal. But make no mistake, we were in a combat zone. And if the continuous sights of up-armored High Mobility Multipurpose Wheeled Vehicles (HMMWVs) and the roar of Mine Resistant Ambush Protected Vehicles (MRAPs) as they rolled by wasn't convincing enough, the near nightly indirect fire (IDF) attacks on FOB Warrior certainly were.

As my primary role and responsibility was to manage and maintain the strategic communications, relationships, and engagements for the battalion commander and the battalion, I would also be the Officer-in-Charge (OIC) of the Personnel Security Detachment (PSD). Adding to a list of things I never knew existed in the Army, the PSD is essentially the bodyguard or security element for a key leader, planning movements, routes, and even our own tactical missions. And while on paper this was assigned as an additional duty, to me, this was my main and most important responsibility. Ensuring the safety and welfare of the soldiers in my charge and ensuring that we were ready and able to respond to any mission, task, or operation thrown our way.

Which is why I spent countless hours studying the outside city, requesting briefs from the intelligence sections, and doing virtual route recons to see which roads and locations had the most kinetic attacks and learning the various tactics, techniques, and procedures (TTPs) that the previous unit implemented.

There were only about two kilometers from the nearest city building to the center of the FOB. This incredibly short distance coupled with the cover and concealment provided by the urban city buildings along the perimeter made our base a magnet for enemy rockets and mortars, along with the ever-present threat of snipers. And it was only within a day or two of arriving that I witnessed our first salvo of rockets landing within the FOB perimeter near our contained housing units (CHUs)—a shipping container turned into a barracks.

There were generally two kinds of rockets: 81 mm and 107 mm. The former was generally less effective as it was essentially a steel pipe packed with some explosive material and a fuse that hooked up to a washing machine timer. I don't know the exact statistics, but it seemed like these rarely ever functioned properly and were nothing more than a big explosive pipe flying through the sky. They were a nuisance more than a threat. The latter, though, was a much different matter.

The 107 mm rockets, Katyusha Rockets, were first developed and fielded by the Soviet Union, and they were designed to be launched off a multiple launcher system from a modified truck. However, as the Soviet Union fell, the stockpile began to trickle across all of Asia. Eventually, it became a rather common weapon supplied by the likes of Iran and China. When one of these was launched, you knew it. Not only did it have a deafening explosion and deadly kill radius, but the death-dealing whistle of one flying overhead was truly terrifying.

Not to mention, we were also always under threat from routine SAF, vehicle-borne improvised explosive devices (VBIEDs), suicide vests (S-VEST), and more rudimentary improvised explosive devices (IEDs). But the two most common attacks US Forces had received came from RKGs and EFPs.

An RKG, a Ruchnaya Kumulyativnaya Granata, was another Russian-developed weapon that was really nothing more than an impact grenade with a parachute. RKGs would target armored convoys and specifically the gunners sitting in the turrets, maintaining overwatch as they would pass through narrow alleyways and in between city buildings. But the biggest threats that US Forces faced in Iraq were ultimately from EFPs: explosively formed penetrators.

An EFP was an extremely lethal form of an improvised explosive device, where a sheet of metal or steel would be placed on top of a charge, and when triggered, the explosion would cause the sheet to morph into a projectile—becoming a shaped charge—that had devastating effects on both unarmored and armored vehicles alike. The origins of these weapons all had receipts tying them back to Iran and Iranian-backed terrorist groups, led by the now deceased Qassim Soleimani, whom US forces struck and killed in 2020.

I first met the PSD soldiers, my soldiers, when they arrived with the main body of the unit several days after I was already settled. The PSD was a ragtag group of soldiers from across the battalion that subordinate units had provided to fill this unit. It was a mix of males and females, all races and ethnicities, representative of all socioeconomic sects of American society. I recognized a couple of them from being around the battalion back at our home station at Fort Hood, but for the most part, I didn't know them, and they didn't know me. Not the ideal situation to begin to conduct combat and/or advise and assist operations in a combat zone.

It wasn't long after we reconstituted our forces that we began to execute "left seat/right seat" operations with the unit we were replacing. This is a stressful time because this two-week period is essentially the only time that we would have to get as much information from the outgoing unit as possible prior to taking responsibility for the area of operations. It also is the most dangerous. Units tend to operate like knowledge vaults. Everything that the unit does and knows, while theoretically archived on memorandums, reports, and standard operating procedures, is unfortunately compartmentalized in the ever-unreliable brain trust of individuals. Which is why these transition periods between units are so critically important and dangerous.

As we first began to conduct our own operations, I knew, and they knew, that it was going to be a rocky couple of weeks. Trust is inherently the backbone of the military. But unlike respect, which is fundamental to a disciplined organization and in theory comes with rank, trust isn't automatically gained—it's earned. And the first person I had to trust and earn the trust of was Hearn.

Staff Sergeant Hearn was a young, cocky, battle-hardened noncommissioned officer (NCO) who had earned his stripes in the mountains of Afghanistan years earlier. He had an interesting personality, to say the least. When I first met him, we exchanged the same awkward pleasantries that you might expect in a blind date—we asked about each other, where we were both from, etc. When soldiers meet each other, a lot of times, it's like dogs at a dog park. We do a little sniffing trying to size each other up, check out the various patches and badges on our uniforms, and then—just like a canine—almost instantaneously know if we will be friends or foes. Yes, it's very primal, but so is the nature of our business.

It only took a second for Hearn, after shaking my hand, to realize that I was just a bright-eyed kid, eager to learn and just praying not to $@*% up. As I was still wary and nervous like the new kid in a new school, Hearn must have sensed that and immediately reached for the back of my arm and pinched the ever-living shit out of me. It was legitimately the hardest "horse bite" pinch I'd had since I was a kid on the playground at St. Jude. And while I overly dramatically cried out in utter surprise, he just cackled his ass off in front of everyone—my boss included. And while certainly not doctrinal and definitely unconventional, his little juvenile prank immediately broke the ice, and like an old dog and a puppy at a dog park, he let me know that he would watch out for me and began showing me the ropes. I immediately knew I was in good hands. Now if only I could live up to my end of the bargain.

Chapter 8

NOT ANOTHER WAR STORY

Our platoon, with the call sign "Titans," easily had one of the highest operational tempos (OPTEMPO) in our battalion; meaning, we were busy as shit. Our commander was very much of the mindset of being present, accessible, and visible both to our allies and partners, as well as our enemies. In six months, we conducted over 120 combat patrols: nearly one patrol a day. And while our patrols may have been only four or five hours at a time, the prep work that goes into them makes for long days in the motor pools for soldiers and even longer nights for me planning the next day's "adventure."

Spending hours on the road day after day, conducting mounted patrols in our HMMWVs—"Humvees"—means that at a certain point, while you're focused on calling out suspicious vehicles or potential IEDs, it's only human nature to begin to have side-bar conversations about, well, random shit: "truck talk." My driver during this deployment was an English kid named Flores. He was an English citizen who moved to America and enlisted in the United States Army with the hopes of securing American citizenship. And as we found out, he was also one hell of a boxer.

My gunner was a kid named Simkins. He was a smart and stoic kid. We would have some interesting and long conversations about the merits of our mission, current international events, and then of course juvenile discussions about random stuff across the battalion. Sometimes he would switch out with another guy named Copeland. Copeland had an enforcer-like personality among the unit and was a rough around the edges guy, but he certainly proved that he was one of the best leaders in our platoon.

While our platoon was a ragtag group, the one thing that we all had in common was that during our very little off time, there was one of two places you could find the PSD: either in the mess hall or the gym. Whether it was a true desire to work out or just the peer pressure of wanting to conform, nearly every day at the same time, the entire Titan Platoon would en masse take over the little FOB Warrior gym. Nothing fosters teamwork and camaraderie like some "sweat equity" with your brothers and sisters in arms.

I don't remember who exactly came up with the idea, I think it was Copeland, but on one of our hours-long patrols, it was brought up that we should have a boxing night. And Flores, the boxer, should teach a class. What started as a rambling idea between soldiers became a reality when nearly our entire unit donned gloves and began doing boxing workouts together. We'd start off rotating through stations, heavy bags, speed bags, and various high-intensity cardio exercises, and then finish with some light sparring—"light" being a very subjective term. For the soldiers, it was a way to let off some steam with each other. The stresses of our patrols and OPTEMPO certainly took their toll, and this was a release of sorts for them. And for me, it was an opportunity to show off a bit and prove to them that I got an "A" in boxing class at West Point, the only "A" I got my entire time there.

Aside from being a good time, our little boxing sessions began to forge deep bonds among the soldiers and, most importantly and ironically, build trust. Trust isn't just the notion of having faith that someone will do a task; to me, it's an underlying belief that the person across from you has a vested interest in you and that they will put your interests above their own. It's a fundamental principle that, unfortunately, we don't see much anymore. And over the course of several weeks of our late-night boxing smokers, the bonds that began to form were tangible. Even as we were punching each other in the face.

Later, I jokingly challenged the same guys in my truck to run the FOB Warrior half marathon that was being held on base; yes, we had marathons at the base, and yes, it was the Air Force unit that organized it. It started out as a joke, but wouldn't you know it, not only did the guys in my truck accept my challenge, but nearly our entire platoon showed up, ran, and finished it. While that in and of itself is not indicative of much, looking back now at the old photo of our platoon after running 13.1 miles in grueling heat on our day off—having not trained—but simply doing it together to do it together, it spoke volumes of the team that we built and the bonds that we forged.

Holidays deployed are always a tough time. Although we do our best to bring a sense of normalcy to our troops, for instance putting Christmas lights on a Humvee and driving it around the FOB or having "Secret Santa" events where every gift is a tin of tobacco, you simply can't replicate what it means to be home. But we try.

In December 2010, our commander received a rather strange request through the Department of State from The Holy See, the Vatican. A couple of months earlier, the Al-Qaeda (AQ) aligned Islamic State in Iraq (ISI)—a precursor to the Islamic State in the Levant (ISIL) and Islamic State in Iraq and Syria (ISIS)—attacked a Chaldean Church service in Baghdad. The attack killed fifty-eight people and garnered widespread global condemnation from across the religious community and faith centers. However, ISI doubled down on their actions in an audio message claiming responsibility for the attack and then called for a jihad—"holy war"—against Christians, Christian centers, and anyone supporting them. So, when this message was relayed, for the commander, it came as a bit of a surprise, but I was not shocked. The request in the message from the Vatican was simple: protect the Christians during Christmas.

It's estimated that in 2010, there were over 300,000 Chaldean Catholics living in Iraq. And while the preponderance was reportedly living in Baghdad, the implied task as relayed from the Department of State was to ensure that Archbishop Louis Raphaël I Sako, the Archbishop of Kirkuk, and his Church were secured during the holiday season. Having been in the country for several months at this point in the wild world of Kirkuk, nothing seemed too strange or too out of the norm anymore.

After several rounds of calls between our interpreters and Archbishop Sako's representatives, our battalion formulated plans to provide a dedicated Quick Response Force (QRF) along checkpoints around the church. The mere presence of soldiers patrolling the streets would hopefully be enough to deter any nefarious actors from attacking the church or parishioners. But then came another request: the archbishop wanted to meet us, face to face.

A day or two before Christmas, we mounted our vehicles with our command team and chaplain and drove to meet the archbishop at his church. We had to pass through the various US military checkpoints around the perimeter; it was a bit of an eerie feeling to imagine passing through checkpoints manned by armed soldiers to go to Christmas mass. As we pulled up out front of the church, which was a rather nondescript building from the exterior, our vehicles pulled into a herringbone formation—a type of security posture—with our mounted .50 caliber machine guns arrayed in interlocking sectors of fire. One of the requests from the local priest whom we coordinated with was that we not bring any weapons into the church. The good Catholic schoolboy in me wanted to abide by this request, but the reality of the situation and my responsibility meant that I couldn't take that risk. So, we met in the middle. I told him that we wouldn't bring any rifles into the church, but we had to carry our standard issue 9 mm Beretta pistols.

Walking into the church was a heavy moment. Because while we were in awe of the beautiful tapestries and murals covering the ancient walls, hidden from the outside world, it was unavoidable to think that the Christians in this church were under direct threat simply for being Christians. Religious terrorism is nothing new to the world, but for me, this was the first time I was in close enough proximity to feel it.

Sitting with the archbishop and several of his fellow priests, among the permeating fear, there was also a sense of calm and peace. I don't know if it was because of the dozens of armed soldiers manning checkpoints outside the perimeter, or the several of us in the room—wearing body armor and carrying side arms—but looking back I think it was certainly something more. And while I keep my own religious beliefs closely held, the faith and conviction that the clergy had, to them, was greater protection than anything our forces could have provided.

After that meeting, the archbishop thanked us and then handed us all a small Chaldean cross: a memento to some and the most impenetrable body armor to others. As we mounted our vehicles to continue with the patrol that night, the guys in my truck asked me how it was and what happened—as they always did. But instead of telling jokes and making light of what normally is a long-winded and wasteful hour or two of drinking tea and talking about bullshit, this time I was almost at a loss for words.

Soldiers in the military sometimes tend to think of themselves as sheepdogs, protecting the flock and ready to do violence on their behalf. But maybe that wasn't the right analogy. Maybe the archbishop and his clergy were the real sheepdogs. And maybe, in some way, we were the wolves? I questioned a lot in the following days of that engagement: my role, our mission, and why we were there in Iraq in the first place. Finally, I found myself questioning my own faith, or should I say my lack thereof.

After the holidays and thankfully without any "spectacular attacks"—yes, that's a real term—we continued the grind of daily patrols, missions, and tea times with our "friends." I use that term loosely because while we considered members of the Iraqi Security Force (ISF) to be our allies and partners, we also knew of much of the corruption going on behind the scenes. While in theory the image of Americans patrolling the streets should provide a sense of calm and collective security, what we found out all too often is that people see that image as an opportunity to line their pockets courtesy of "Uncle Sam."

As part of our strategy was still under the auspices of "winning the hearts and minds" of the people of Iraq, a program was established called the Commander's Emergency Response Program (CERP). This was a program established around 2005 or 2006 that was to be used to rebuild humanitarian and civil infrastructure in both Iraq and Afghanistan. From the US perspective, it was seen as an opportunity to leverage good deeds to win favor with the local populace and deter nefarious actors. It was nothing more than a cash grab by locals.

By 2010 or 2011, nearly all our senior ISF partners knew about this program as it had doled out an estimated $2 billion, and every so often they would drop hints about trying to get projects allocated in their districts or towns—not very different from our own government. And as luck would have it, I was tasked with putting together one such project in one of the districts. Another random assignment that I was thoroughly not trained for, educated on, or even remotely qualified for.

As the new CERP project manager, I began working with our battalion engineer to determine the size and scope of this project. How much money did we have, what projects made sense, and what would have the largest return on investment (ROI) both for the beneficiaries and for the US forces. With a little guidance, and some heavy-handed steering from our Iraqi partners, it was agreed upon that instead of building a clinic or a school—something of real value—we were going to refurbish a local vendor's marketplace store. My skeptical nature immediately raised red flags: "…Wait, we're doing what? For whom?"

The project was approved through the right bureaucratic channels and the funding allocated. We made a couple of trips out to meet the shopkeeper and discuss the project and what the funds would be used for. He showed us his convenience store–sized shop and explained how he was going to build out a refrigerated storage room with it. This would allow him to keep more perishable food items on hand for the local community. I thought to myself, "… Okay, maybe this isn't such a scam…"

Then the day came when we would deliver the funds to him. While a rather routine thing in the grand scheme of Operations Iraqi Freedom and New Dawn—the Iraqi campaign names from 2003 to 2011—when we showed up with a large bag of cash, our ISF partner was there waiting for us as well. After some initial pleasantries, we handed over the cash, took a couple photos, and discussed the follow-up things that we would need to ensure that the money was used correctly. But during that protocol, and maybe through an unintended slip of the tongue, it just happened to be revealed that the shopkeeper was coincidentally a cousin of one of our ISF partners. I don't know if that was the turning point for me, but it certainly was a "What the $@*% are we doing here?" moment.

The longer we were in Iraq, the more that sentiment seemed to grow. Like a virus, it began infecting all of us. Where we, as leaders, could normally play it off by talking about the importance of the mission, the good stuff we were doing, the terrorists we were capturing or killing, or the lives we were saving, that slowly began to fade. And I found myself questioning what our real goals were in Iraq. Yes, we were advising and assisting the ISF, but everyone knew that once we left—which was written in stone because of the end of the Status of Forces Agreement (SOFA)—everything that we had built and every sacrifice that far too many had given was potentially all for naught.

Meanwhile, we still had a job to do. We would go on patrol, day after day, in a real-life game of whack-a-mole. The problem was, were we the "whackers" or were we the moles? Keeping morale up and maintaining good order and discipline became increasingly tough in those days. But that's not to say that our soldiers weren't ready to protect themselves, each other, and itching to do violence on behalf of a grateful nation. Not to mention, back home, the domestic turbulence of political theatrics just added to the fire of depleted morale for our troops.

The military is famously and fundamentally apolitical. And rightfully so. One of the most important aspects of our military is that it is led by civilians as outlined in the United States Constitution in what is often referred to as the "civilian control of the military" principle. And this separation, or isolation, of the military from domestic politics is vital to the good order and discipline that we must have as soldiers. And is a fundamental aspect to ensuring that regardless of administrations, or who is in any elected office, that the American public can trust that the Armed Forces of the United States will continue to honor their oath "to support and defend the Constitution of the United States against all enemies." But, and this is a very fine line, every person, regardless of whether you're a normal civilian or a service member in uniform, is entitled to their own opinion and does have the right to free speech—with limitations.

So as our collective morale was sinking incredibly, when word got out that there may be a government shutdown in the spring of 2011, that wasn't just throwing gasoline on a fire, but it was driving a semi laden with C4 explosives right into the black zone of the flame. Granted, we didn't really know what it meant, but surely it would have implications for those of us half a world away in Iraq.

Rumors began to fly around, and there were more questions than answers. The general sentiment that we heard during random run-ins with other officers at the mess hall was "there's no way the government will shut down, and if it does, there's absolutely no way they won't pay us. We're in Iraq for $@*%'s sake." But that was all conjecture. Emails began to circulate informing soldiers of potential pay delays, offering support and services. And while that's all fine and dandy, the fact is that most soldiers live paycheck to paycheck. Now add in the fact that behind that one soldier is potentially a family, a spouse, children, relying on that paycheck for basic life support such as food on the table and a roof over their heads.

In 2021, the nonprofit Feeding America reported that approximately 125,000 service members face food insecurity— defined by them as a "lack of consistent access to food supply for every person in a household." So, missing a paycheck or even having it delayed is a huge burden that my soldiers should not have even had to fathom let alone face. But the reality was that there was absolutely nothing any of us, thousands of miles away, could do. The nightmare scenario that this would cause all hinged on decisions being made thousands of miles away by groups of people who more than likely never served in uniform, and almost certainly had no idea the ramifications of their meddling: the United States Congress.

As the deadline for the shutdown grew closer, Hearn and I began to ask soldiers how it would affect them and what, if anything, we could do to help them if this unfathomable event happened. For kids in combat with families back home, this was and is the absolute last thing they should have been forced to deal with. But there we were, talking to our soldiers about their families' budgets, making sure that their kids had food in the pantry and enough money to keep the lights on. I was absolutely disgusted.

One of our soldiers, he was a new kid, a young private, had just gotten to us a couple months earlier. For the sake of privacy, I'll refer to him as Smith. Smith joined the army shortly after having a newborn with his wife. Now, one of the benefits of serving in combat—if there are any—is that Uncle Sam doesn't take any taxes out of basic pay; it's called the combat zone tax exclusion. And while it's a nice benefit for some, for a private making approximately $1,900 per month, barely above the poverty threshold, it's negligible.

We could have done a lot of things. We could have berated him for blowing all his money, we could have lectured him about living outside his means, or we could have even investigated his monthly budget and account statements to see exactly what was occurring. But we didn't do any of that. Instead, Hearn and I looked at each other, and without hesitation or question asked each other, "So how much money do you have right now and how much does your family need?" Without flinching, Hearn and I were about to pay his bills and rent, buy his groceries, and do what it took to ensure that his family would be safe and financially secure. It wasn't even a second thought for us.

Thankfully, the government didn't shut down, and the paychecks weren't delayed, and so on and so forth. In full transparency, later we found out that if a shutdown had occurred, there were provisions in it to continue to pay military service members, etc. But that information was all gained in hindsight. And although the calamity of this mess ultimately was avoided, the disdain that had been festering about our mission, our jobs, and our role in Iraq was exacerbated by this bullshit politicking happening back home.

Later that spring, I was moved to another job within the battalion, and my friend Taylor Force took over my role and numerous duty titles. Taylor was my West Point classmate, and while I didn't know him at the Academy, he and I went to Fort Sill together and were now stationed together in the same battalion. He was legitimately the nicest person I've ever met, with an infectious smile and a laugh that could make the direst circumstances lighthearted. We had become fast friends when we got to the unit the year previously, and with him taking over the team, I knew that my soldiers were in good hands and that he was in good hands as well.

The deployment for me was seemingly over. I was now relegated to a desk job on the base and quickly became one of the people that I jokingly referred to early on, working a regular day job, proverbially punching in, and punching out. It was a hard adjustment for me to go from running on empty for nearly seven months straight to barely running at all. I tried to live vicariously through Taylor and would swing by at night to catch up while he was writing reports or while he was planning for the next mission. He'd tell me jokes about the guys, or funny things that happened along the way.

I missed the PSD platoon. I'd see them around occasionally, either getting ready to go out on the streets or just coming back from a mission. Sometimes I'd see them in the gym wearing the custom Titan Platoon shirts we got everyone for Christmas. And not a day went by that I didn't wish that I was there with them. For as many bad things that happened, for as many precarious situations that we were in, every time I think back to Iraq, all I think about are our soldiers, my soldiers.

Chapter 9

REVOLUTIONS AND REVELATIONS

In 2011, a Tunisian merchant named Mohamed Bouazizi, a regular street vendor selling produce from a wheel barrel, was accosted by Tunisian police who seized both his produce and his money. He had reportedly been the target of Tunisian authorities for years and, unable to bribe his way out of this most recent altercation, was publicly humiliated by the police.

Mohamed went to the local governor's office to file an official complaint. Upon arriving at the governor's office, he was then summarily turned away and refused to be seen by any members or officials of the Tunisian government. In response, he procured some gasoline, walked into the middle of a busy street, doused himself, and then lit a fire that not only consumed him but lit the spark for the reformation movement known as the "Arab Spring."

Protests broke out in nearly every Middle Eastern country because of the images of Bouazizi's self-immolation. But the main focal point for the Arab Spring was in Egypt. There, the protests began on January 25, 2011, a date coinciding with an Egyptian holiday honoring police, and the grievances were primarily aimed at Egyptian President Hosni Mubarak and his regime's brutality against its citizens. Images from Tahrir square, ground zero for the Egyptian revolution, captured the imaginations of millions of people living under oppression both in the region and across the world.

In the southern Syrian city of Dar'a (Daraa)—where nearly a century earlier Lawrence of Arabia conducted clandestine reconnaissance operations against the Ottoman Empire—young Syrians also took to the streets just as they'd seen their peers do on social media across the Middle East. Building on the scenes and successes they had seen in Tunisia, Egypt, and across the Levant, Syrians seized the moment and movement. But in Dar'a, unlike in other cities, the movement would take a drastic turn and ultimately destroy a country, millions of lives, and the futures for generations of people.

In March 2011, a group of Syrian teenagers were detained for painting gratffii on a school in Dar'a denouncing President Bashar al-Assad and his oppressive regime. Reports began circulating that the detained boys were being beaten while in Syrian custody, and with no new information on their condition or a timeline for their release, the families of the teenagers along with hundreds of Syrian citizens took to the streets to protest the unjust treatment for this petty crime, chanting "God, Syria, Freedom."

Later that month Syrian Regime forces encircled the city in an effort to isolate the protests from spreading. And on March 24, 2011, dozens of protesters were killed when the regime opened fire on the largely peaceful crowd. If Mohamed Bouazizi lit the revolutionary fuse of the Arab Spring in Tunisia, al-Assad's own actions threw gasoline on it in Syria.

As the weeks turned into months, and al-Assad strengthened his grip on the citizens of Syria, he fired his cabinet ministers, placed blame on foreign conspirators for the protests, and committed to a full-throated crackdown on civil unrest through mobilized military power. In response, the once loosely organized civil disturbance had become a rather codified military organization aptly named the Free Syrian Army (FSA). The FSA included defectors from the Syrian Armed Forces and protestors alike, taking on the mission of defending unarmed civilians from their own government with the ambitious end state to overthrow al-Assad. The Syrian civil unrest morphed into an all-out civil war.

Meanwhile, as all hell was breaking loose in Syria, I was on a flight back from Iraq. My dad flew from Florida to Texas to be there when I get back. He dropped me off the day we flew out for our deployment, so it was only right that he came and picked me up too. The euphoria of coming back from deployment with the streets lined with American flags and the pomp and circumstance associated with the military ceremonies was only eclipsed by one thing, my hunger. After flying out of Kirkuk to another base in Iraq, to Kuwait, with a quick pit stop in Ireland, I was ravenous. So, while it was obviously great to see my dad, I was even more elated when the first question he asked me was "So are you hungry?" Without missing a beat, and before putting my bags down, or even getting a hot shower, we were sitting at the International House of Pancakes in Killeen, Texas, still in the sweat-stained uniform I'd been wearing for days, as I ate my body weight in fluffy pancakes.

Our unit was replaced with the 1st Battalion, 5th Field Artillery Regiment (1-5 FA), nicknamed "Hamilton's Own" in honor of the first commander Captain Alexander Hamilton. One of the oldest if not the oldest units in the army, 1-5 FA would essentially close out operations at FOB Warrior, as December 31, 2011, was the end date for Operation New Dawn per failed SOFA negotiations with GoI. After nearly a decade of continuous combat operations in Iraq, and thousands of sacrifices, it would all be over.

After the honeymoon of returning home, I began to deal with several personal "readjustment issues." For one thing, I was on edge and on guard nearly every moment every day. Walking down the sidewalk outside my apartment in Austin, I was constantly scanning the ground for IEDs. I would always ensure that my back was to a corner, and that I had a clear line of sight to the main doorway or entryway of any room I was in. If a person was walking up to me, I immediately looked to see where their hands were and if there might be some weapon or explosive underneath their clothing. And if there was any sudden loud noise, a door slam, a dropped glass, I would immediately have a visible fight-or-flight reaction. The only consolation with this was that I wasn't the only one dealing with these issues.

My disdain with how things in Iraq went and knowing exactly how they were eventually going to turn out began to grow. Whereas early on I thought that our efforts there could have made a difference, now, back home, resettled and readjusting, I looked at it as an entire waste. A waste of time, a waste of treasure, and a waste of American lives. Thankfully, no one from our unit was killed in combat, but my heart was heavy for all the families and friends for the thousands who were killed in the nearly decade-long war. I wondered if they would ever find solace in their loved one's sacrifice.

While I was battling the rocky road of adjusting to my "new normal," my inner demons began to have a heavier say in my personal affairs. I began going out too much, partying too hard, drinking too much, and frankly, living too recklessly. I compartmentalized all these risky things under the banner of "I'm just making up for lost time," but I was dealing with things much darker and deeper. Then in early November, I got news that rocked me to my core.

Dustin Vincent, from 1-5 FA, who I met during our transition out of Iraq and who took the same position that both Taylor and I had held, was killed by a sniper in Kirkuk. The details were hard to come by, but the information I received from people there was that Dustin was on a routine patrol along one of the routes we drove. They dismounted their vehicles at some point, and from one of the buildings, a sniper took a shot that ultimately took his life. It crushed me. I immediately found myself back in Iraq. Thinking of what I could have done differently to mitigate that risk or to potentially prevent it. Did we miss something? Did we not do a good enough job? Did I not give 1-5 FA a good enough handover? What could I have done differently? These were all thoughts that just kept percolating for days and weeks on end.

I had a serious girlfriend several months after we got back from Iraq, and even in the short time that we dated, she could tell that something wasn't right. The drinking wasn't just social, it was excessive, and it was an escape. The emotional swings from happiness to rage to depressive sadness shifted like the winds. But this wasn't just me. Several of my friends had rather similar experiences. So, when we'd get together, and someone got into a fight or, more often than not, one of the boys was in the corner with his head on the bar crying, it normalized this for us. When we should have been thinking, "Dude, what the $@*% is wrong with us?" we were instead thinking, "Eh, he's just drunk."

I had been a good officer, received good evaluations, and after proving myself downrange, garnered praise and accolades from my superiors. And while I had set my own personal bar rather high, and because of my performance, others expected more out of me, but now back home I had become an absolute trainwreck of a leader and shitshow of a soldier. On the outside, I was self-absorbed, detached, unfocused, lackadaisical, aloof, and downright selfish. But on the inside, well, that's a whole different story.

I was once again on another out-of-control downward spiral, except this time I was old enough to know better but young—and damaged—enough to simply not care.

Chapter 10

CROSSING RED LINES

In the summer of 2013, I received orders to report to Fort Bliss, Texas. I had just spent another stint at Fort Sill, Oklahoma, going through an advanced officer course: "Captain's Career Course." Frankly, the course, the program, and the leadership—not all, by any means—were terrible. And after submitting a list of preferable next assignments for my next career move as an Army officer, I received none of them; I even put Fort Benning on there—and combat arms folks know to never put Fort Benning on any potential assignment list. Adding that last slight onto an already long laundry list of disdain, and I was done.

I already made the decision to pull my packet from going to Special Forces Assessment and Selection (SFAS), and this next assignment was the last straw for me; it was time to leave the military. I had good leaders and I had terrible ones, exceptional soldiers and lackluster ones, and great assignments and miserable jobs. But at the time, all I could think about was the negativity of my career, and not the positive moments and good times. Instead of reliving the days in the field with our troops, the joy that comes with helping a soldier succeed in whatever their personal or professional goal is, and the sense of belonging that comes with simply being a part of a team, that was all overshadowed by my own personal professional grievances and selfishness.

This negativity also permeated my personal life. Coupled with the struggles I continued to deal with, in totality, I was miserable, unhappy, and angry. And unfortunately, and regretfully, I began isolating myself from friends, family, and loved ones. I felt alone on an island, and my pride didn't allow me to send out an SOS.

During this same time, half a world away, the Syrian Civil War continued to escalate. Now in its second year, it had become a full force-on-force civil war, engaging a host of actors including nefarious violent extremist groups aligned with Al Qaeda (AQ). Additionally, open-source reports began circulating earlier in 2013 that the Syrian Regime, under al-Assad, had not only stockpiled and planned to use chemical weapons, but that they already had. Given the remarks President Obama gave on August 20, 2012, during a press conference from the Brady Press Room at the White House, the world believed that action would soon follow.

"We have been very clear to the Assad regime, but also to other players on the ground, that a red line for us is we start seeing a whole bunch of chemical weapons moving around or being utilized. That would change my calculus. That would change my equation." – President Obama

Then on August 28, 2013, over a year since his statement and following months of accusations, video footage, and assessments from both US and international organizations confirming that Syria had indeed used chemical weapons, President Obama confirmed these allegations stating while on PBS NewsHour: "We have concluded that the Syrian Government in fact carried [chemical weapon strikes] out…" While my own personal red line had been crossed and my decision to leave the military was final, on paper, the rest of the world's red line regarding Syria had also been crossed.

My assignment at Fort Bliss was within the Headquarters

of the 1st Armored Division (1st AD), serving as the sometimes acting, sometimes assistant Fire Support Officer. This meant that I was in meetings with Division Staff way above my pay grade and experience. But this was not a completely foreign place to be. I had semi-mastered the art of the notion "fake it 'til you make it" in Iraq, so I was sure it would work here too. And as luck would have it, in 2013, under then Army Chief of Staff General Ray Odierno, 1st AD was selected as the regionally aligned force for US Central Command (CENTCOM), the same global combatant command that oversaw the entire Middle East. Meaning, as Syria was escalating, 1st AD was the first conventional force provider to respond. Perfect timing for me.

I spent the time between Obama's announcement and confirmation on several iterations of training between the field and command post exercises at Fort Bliss, and then a stint at the National Training Center (NTC) near Death Valley, California. All in preparation for that one fateful call around Thanksgiving: "Captain DeMarco, you're getting orders to deploy to Jordan."

A week or two later, after packing up my belongings into a dusty storage unit in El Paso, Texas, I was lying on a hammock in the cargo hold on a C-130, touching down at a small Jordanian military base in virtually the center of the capital city, Amman. Our group of about a dozen soldiers and civilians from Fort Bliss quickly got off the C-130 ramp and went to the nearby trailer, which served as a de facto customs house. It was here that our official passports were stamped and where we begin to understand the dynamic of our time in the Hashemite Kingdom of Jordan.

From what I surmised, the Department of Defense was requested to have a small and relatively invisible presence in Jordan because of the Syrian Civil War. The US didn't have the best reputation in the region because of our swift exit from Iraq, so this wasn't just a safety or force protection issue but moreover a political one. We deployed under Title 22, which meant that while we reported to our senior leaders, commanding general, and ultimately the secretary of defense and president, it was the US ambassador in Amman who still had charge of US military forces in Jordan. So, even though we were technically in a combat zone, receiving hostile fire and imminent danger pay, the reality was it was anything but combat.

We were based at the King Abdullah II Special Operations Training Center (KASOTC), a large training base on the outskirts of Amman, with the mission to provide world-class training to special operators from across the region. As guests at KASOTC, which I was almost positive was largely built with and by the United States, we lived and worked under many local customs, courtesies, and rules. Additionally, while technically deployed, I quickly realized that the steady state battle rhythm of CENTCOM Forward-Jordan (CF-J) included briefings in the morning, sports in the evening, and traveling the historic and ancient biblical lands on the weekends. But who was I to judge? I indulged in my fair share of floating in the Dead Sea with a fruity cocktail and hookah every now and then as well because who wouldn't? For the record I also dipped my toe in the Jordan River and didn't melt and hiked the trails of Wadi Mujib and didn't turn into salt.

My initial assignment at CF-J was going to be an assistant to an assistant operations planner, a stereotypical staffer, a typical position for a young captain at CF-J. However, as luck would have it, as another captain was set to rotate out—leave the deployment—as I was rotating in—arriving—that meant there was a billet needing to be filled. And as just another number, with a relatively high ranking on the alphabet roster, I was diverted to join the Military Engagement Team Jordan (MET-J). That sounded great,

I thought. But then another familiar internal voice said, "What the $@*% is the MET-J?"

The MET-J was a small team led by a National Guard unit from a specific state—in this case Washington—and augmented with several assets such as intelligence professionals, a Civil Affairs team, and Special Forces operators. Their mission was to liaise and partner with the Jordanian Armed Forces, specifically the Border Guard, to provide capability-enhancing products, assessments, and information. Being essentially landlocked between Israel, Syria, and Iraq, Jordan has historically been concerned with its northern border, and given the current situation with the civil war and the second- and third-order effects associated, such as the Syrian refugee migration and crises, it was in everyone's best interest that MET-J focused efforts on that AO. While the MET-J supported this mission, because of various political considerations, personally assigned weapons like an M4 rifle or M9 pistol were not authorized, and neither were uniforms. On paper the team was a military unit, but we were no more prepared than a humanitarian organization traversing some of the most dangerous conflict areas in the Middle East.

One of the projects that the MET-J was involved with was providing geographical survey information to the Border Guard. This meant that our team would travel all over the country and survey border locations to provide Jordanians both a digital common operating picture—basically a Google map with plotted security post positions—along with recommendations on gaps in their security or potential areas of smuggling, trafficking, etc. Because of our ability to move freely about the country, and the nearly unrestricted access we had to the northern border, our unit was effectively one of the only Department of Defense assets that was able to provide insight into what was occurring just over the border in Syria.

Adam D. DeMarco

From our safe vantage point, we'd watch as smoke rose over nearby cities as the Syrian Army launched missiles from aircraft and dropped indiscriminate barrel bombs from helicopters. Then hours later, we'd be there as the civilian casualties from those attacks were driven or sometimes carried to the border location where the Jordanians set up casualty collection points with fully equipped medical facilities. We'd watch, helplessly, as scores of men, women, and children would arrive with what can only be described as the most graphic wounds of war. Some would make it, others wouldn't. The bodies of those who were killed were then wrapped in shrouds, rolled into rugs, put in the back of a van, and sent away to be immediately buried as is customary and in accordance with Islamic law.

On one specific occasion, a child was brought across. He was probably seven years old. He was screaming in agony and his face and head were covered in blood. I assume it was his father who was carrying him into the medical tent, but I never found out. Our interpreter, Kamal, went over to a nearby Jordanian who was at the entrance of the tent to ask about his condition. A little while later, I saw the same child being carried out of the tent by the same man. But when I saw the child, he was no longer screaming. He was silent. He was limp. He was dead. Kamal looked at me and just shook his head. Another victim of war.

To their credit, the Jordanian military and the countless volunteers assisting on the border proved that in the worst of situations, there is still goodness to be had and made. Spending many nights with them, in the deserts of Wadi Rum and along the northern borders, I found myself falling in love with their culture. Looking back, I think that many of the qualities and values that I saw in the people of the Hashemite Kingdom were the same ones that T. E. Lawrence must have seen and embodied on his journey to become Lawrence of Arabia.

One evening we were up near the Golan Heights and the Sea of Galilee, on the northwestern corner where Jordan, Israel, and Syria meet. We had a couple of meetings with the Border Guard in what was a beautiful valley covered in green foliage—much different from the Mars-like areas in the south. After meeting with our partners, ever the gracious hosts, they wanted to show us "something." I didn't hear what it was, or where we were going, but I hopped in the very back of our Ford Expedition and off we went. The sun was beginning to set so in my mind this would be our last stop before heading back to KASOTC.

We followed the Border Guard escort down several winding roads into a valley where there was a cleared area with a trail leading up the other adjacent mountain into Syria. This was, as we quickly found out, a nondescript and clandestine border crossing. There were several vehicles already there, a couple on the Jordanian side and a couple on the Syrian side. It almost looked like a car rally or meet up of sorts, a bunch of people just waiting around for Vin Diesel to show up in his muscle car.

Our Jordanian partners exited their vehicles and approached the non-delineated border and began speaking with the other group. As we, the Americans, were both guests and unarmed, we slowly exited the vehicles but kept our wary distance. As we were now in the middle of a valley, darkness quickly engulfed us, and visibility was extremely limited. However, after several minutes of waiting, we then saw a van driving down the opposing trail—the trail that led from Syria to our meeting point. As the lights of the van shined down the winding trail, we began to see other people along the trail. Because they were clad in all black, we hadn't seen them before, but the dimly lit lights of the van compromised their positions.

As the van pulled up, we quickly figured out this was another patient transfer. But what about the people on the road? The guys in all black, who were they? We asked one of the Jordanians near us, and he casually brushed it off, saying that they were Syrians. The patient was then loaded into a Jordanian ambulance that had come by, and we were asked to follow them to the hospital. This was a bit different now, as we weren't sure exactly what we were doing or why we were there. But we followed along.

When we got to the hospital, which was on much friendlier and safer terrain, I was unsatisfied with the answer that "they're just Syrians." I'm not an intelligence analyst, but we all had enough knowledge of the area of operations to know of the varying dynamics at play and the multitudes of organizations operating in the area. So, not content with the first answer, I went back to the same Jordanian Border Guard and asked him again—through our interpreter, of course—and this time, perhaps because of the serious look in my face, the sternness of my translated question, or his just not wanting to deal with the American anymore, I got the real answer: "Al-Nusra."

Jabhat al-Nusra was an AQ aligned and affiliated violent extremist organization that formed in 2012 as a rebel group against the Syrian Army. But then in 2013, it joined forces with AQ and became the predominant rebel force in Syria. And while we couldn't necessarily see them from our vantage point in the valley, they could definitely see us.

It was a weird feeling, though. To now know that we had been outgunned, outmanned, and absolutely in an unfavorable terrain and position. I sometimes wonder why the Jordanian Border Guard officer initially lied. Did he think that we would have done something? Or did he think he was protecting us? I'll never know what the impetus was for him to lie to us, but maybe it was both?

After all, Al-Nusra was engaged in fighting the Syrian Regime, and we were supporting the FSA, who Al-Nusra was also fighting with. Sun Tzu famously stated that "the enemy of my enemy is my friend." And while we certainly will never consider those violent extremists groups friends, seeing the enemy up close and personal to that degree made me realize that while we always focus on what differentiates us—nationalities, beliefs, race—if you boil all those arbitrary differences down, we all have one major commonality: we are all humans.

And while Al-Nusra and AQ were certainly enemies of the United States, it was even weirder to think that they were in a fight that nearly the entire world thought to be a "just war"—meaning a war that is morally justifiable through a series of criteria, all of which must be met for a war to be considered. In an area of the world as fractured and fractioned as the Middle East, being in that valley that day was a humbling experience. Not only because they could have easily killed us, but because it made me realize how gray the gray areas of war can really be. And while the enemy of my enemy wasn't and isn't my friend, it might have been a tacitly understood agreement of non-aggression, as we were for all intents and purposes on the same side for a brief period in time, the side of humanity.

Jordan never seemed to disappoint, as one of the more progressive and modernized countries in the Middle East and a relatively safe and peaceful country. However, it still had some areas where Western culture is for all intents and purposes banned, places we were absolutely forbidden from going to or through. Take the city of Ma'an, for instance.

Ma'an is a couple hundred kilometers south of Amman and sits at the intersection of two of the three north-south running highways from Saudi Arabia back to the capital. Our survey team was tasked to go spend some time on the southern border shared with Saudi Arabia to finish our project, and in preparation for this weeklong mission, we did our proper due diligence. I planned the route, assembled the team, had the embassy secure our lodging—which was one of the nicest resorts in Aqaba—and prepared the equipment for what should have been a solid week of surveying and sunbathing on the Red Sea.

The week went off without a hitch. We spent lots of time driving around Wadi Rum, drinking chai with Bedouins, smoking hookah in Aqaba, and always keeping a watchful eye for some historic ruins from one of Lawrence of Arabia's camps. Alas, the day came when we'd have to venture nearly the entire length of Jordan to get back to our camp. But there was one place we needed to hit first, and it was the farthest east we could have gone, on the eastern side of Wadi Rum, the Al Mudawara Border Crossing, one of the major border crossings for the annual Hajj pilgrimage. We planned it for the last day because we knew it would take the longest to get to, and from there we could essentially head straight back to Amman. But there was one potential problem: we'd be driving near Ma'an.

The reason why that was a problem, and why it was blacklisted, is because it is home to the Salafist movement in Jordan—that is an ultra-conservative radical group bent on pious reformation through social action and, unfortunately, jihadism. In 2002–2003, Salafists clashed with the Jordanian government, which left several dead and hundreds wounded. And the sentiment that sparked those clashes surely hadn't died down since then. But I, as the officer in charge, figured that if we stuck to the hardball highways, we could surely bypass the city and be back at KASOTC in time for chow. Boy was I wrong.

I've failed at things many times. So, owning up to a mistake is not something foreign to me. In fact, by this time in my life, I'd become comfortable with giving the generically old "my bad, sir…" response. But this was a $@*% up like none other. The gravity of which didn't come full circle until after we loaded the vehicle for our trip back and realized that not only had I planned a bad route, but I also hadn't forecasted for gas. And you guessed it, the only petrol station we could find was in Ma'an.

There were very few options at this point, and this is one of the few times in my life where I can say that we were all out of good ideas. Assuming tons of risk, we ventured into the de facto capital of radical Jordanian Salafism. Three of us, one guy who looked like Bryan Cranston's character "Heisenberg" from *Breaking Bad*, another who could have been the biological twin of famed professional wrestler Jim "Hacksaw" Dugan, and then me who was once referred to as the doppelgänger for Frankie Muniz in *Malcolm in the Middle*, and our interpreter. What could go wrong?

Chapter 11

INDELIBLE AND UNFORGETTABLE

W e pulled over at the gas station and tried to slink down in our seats as much as possible to avoid being seen. It was the middle of the day, our windows had no tint, and we stood out like, well, three white guys in the Middle East. Our interpreter spoke with the attendant, and after a brief negotiation, we handed him the cash and we were able to fill up. Granted, there were numerous old men sitting around curiously watching us, but not in a threatening manner. They were probably as worried to see us as we were to be there. With our tank full, we then headed back out onto the highway. Disaster averted.

We got back on the highway, and once we cleared the immediate area, we then began to run into traffic. What started as an initial slowdown turned into a sheer gridlock as we approached a roundabout. Crawling up toward it, we could see lots of people massing around the center of the rotary and, as our eyes adjusted to the blinding sun, saw the crowd was all young military-aged males, wearing traditional Salafi garb. We could hear from inside our vehicle that there was a loudspeaker of sorts, maybe a megaphone, that was relaying a speech of some kind. Our interpreter briefly cracked his window to try to hear what was being said to no avail. Regardless, we all immediately knew this wasn't good.

Our car went from what was normally jovial conversation filled with jokes, stories, and music trivia to absolute silence. We inched closer to the rotary, and then began to drive around it. Our driver, the Heisenberg lookalike, tried to maneuver from our lane, which was closest to the inner circle, to the outside lane, which made absolute sense. But in doing so, this caused more attention as the symphony of car horns made clear that something wasn't right and that someone—or some people—was out of place. As we tried to get to the outside lane, now essentially blocking two complete lanes right in front of this mass gathering, eyes began turning our way. And then the feet of those military-aged males began to follow their eyes, and soon we had a crowd walking toward us. This is exactly how nightmares begin.

Heisenberg, without saying a thing, then began to gun the car and immediately hit the brakes. Essentially signaling to everyone around us: "If you don't get out of our way, we will run you the $@*% over." Cars then began to move out of our way, creating barely enough room to walk through let alone get our Ford Expedition through. The clock was running out. I hit the door's lock button several times to make sure that they were indeed locked, and then grabbed the knife I kept in my back pocket. I knew that if it came to it, we were dead but foolishly thought that maybe I could take out a guy or two before we ended up on the Al-Jazeera News.

Dead silence. There was no communication, no talking, no yelling, nothing. The group of military-aged males got closer and closer, yelling, shouting, and pointing, almost close enough for them to grab the door handle. Meanwhile, Heisenberg kept gunning the vehicle toward the other cars. He was able to create some space, and we began to crawl out of the gridlock, but it was a race against time now. I took off my seat belt just in case, looked back at "Hacksaw" who was ready to drop a proverbial two-by-four on the first guy who tried to grab him, and then looked back at Heisenberg who now had is knife out by his left leg as he hit the accelerator and brake with his right. And then I looked back to the left and saw the crowd, they were close enough that I could see both the anger in their eyes and the stains on their teeth. Then, out of the dead silence in the car, I heard the most beautiful sound and felt the most beautifully violent jolt. Our engine revved and accelerated at what felt like Mach-speed levels. Heisenberg was able to maneuver out of the gridlock, and now we were racing down a narrow alleyway, our side view mirrors hitting clothes lines and hanging laundry; it was a scene right out of a generic getaway chase movie. We drove down this alley for what was probably only a minute but felt like a lifetime. I looked back to see if we were being chased—as if the military-aged males had Terminator-like speed—and when it looked like the coast was clear, Heisenberg then made a sharp right-hand turn, and just like that, as quickly as what could have been a jihadi propaganda film in the making, it was over. We were safe, and in the clear, and back on the highway to Amman.

It took a while for the adrenaline to simmer down. Ten minutes must have gone by without anyone saying anything. What was there to say? Did we get attacked? No. Did we almost get attacked? Probably. Would we have been killed? Absolutely. In those moments, we knew that we were vastly outnumbered, and if we did get into a fight, then we were all going to die. There was no question. But there was also no question that we were not going to be captured or kidnapped. These were all thoughts that were running through my head now as I was mentally reflecting and trying to understand what in the hell just almost happened. And while my mind raced just as fast as we drove down that alleyway, our driver, Heisenberg, summed up all our collective thoughts into the single greatest quote I may have ever heard: "Well, boys, that was almost the last great knife fight."

Thankfully, it worked out. After getting a relatively mild "ass chewing" when we got back to KASOTC, I debriefed with our intelligence section and counterintelligence folks to give them the "5-Ws"—who, what, where, when, and why—of what occurred. Needless to say, Ma'an stayed on the blacklist for a while after that. I, in my own way, apologized to our guys about that. It was an unnecessary risk that we took, or better said, that I put them in. As the stalwart professionals they were, they didn't make a big deal out of it, but as the team leader of that mission, everything that we did or failed was my responsibility; and, yes, that even includes almost getting dragged out of a car because we were in a city we were told not to be and potentially executed in public. I wish I could say that was our last run-in with jihadists or violent extremist organizations, but unfortunately that was just the start.

In February of 2014, I was tasked with leading a small team out to a refugee processing center. This team was mixed with civil affairs and intelligence professionals, and our mission was to gain information from newly arriving refugees about what was occurring in Syria, such as where they came from, who was there fighting, what was happening. Our concept was simple: to go to one of the main processing locations that Syrians are taken to—before they are taken to a United Nations refugee camp—and conduct interviews with them. The hope was to get a large amount of data that the intelligence professionals could then analyze and build a common operating picture of Syria. As Syria was a black hole for information, and there were no US forces operating in or around it, the information we gained would be pivotal in determining a future strategy for stakeholders—which included the Department of Defense, the United States Congress, and even up to the National Security Council (NSC) at the White House. Driving out to this processing center, I was sitting shotgun as the song "Once in a Lifetime" played from my iPhone through the speakers of the now beat-up Ford Expedition; it was fitting. We arrived at the processing center, which was in the last small town before hitting the eastern border of Jordan and Iraq. Before we pulled in, we stopped at the little local market and stocked up on Wild Tiger energy drinks and cheap cigarettes—a notion that former Secretary of Defense James Mattis would reportedly bring up in his job interview with President-Elect Donald Trump.

Pulling into the camp, it was divided into two big circus-like tents, and then two buildings that looked like the CHUs we had in Iraq. One tent was for the women and children, the other was for all military-aged males, and then one building was the Jordanian Operations Center, and the other was the one we'd use for lodging. The most recent refugees who arrived had already processed in and were loading up to be bused to the Zaatari refugee camp, which was about an hour west of our location.

Everything at the processing center had been donated either by or through the United Nations High Commissioner for Refugees— the UN Refugee Agency—and as such everything from the broken air conditioners to the wool blankets had a flag of a different country promoting their support of humanitarian operations. Additionally, and while this wasn't a covert or clandestine mission by any stretch of the imagination, it was common practice for us to tell people who we met who were not members of the Jordanian Armed Forces (JAF) that we were Canadians and members of a humanitarian organization. Making our jobs sound dull and boring reduced the prying questions.

The next morning, the first truckload of refugees arrived.

They were trucked in from the nearby border crossing carrying all their earthly possessions on their backs. Men, women, and lots of children piled out of the truck beds and were then separated into the two tents that they would call home for the next couple of days. Normally a tongue-in-cheek saying, but in this case, it was a stark reminder that for many of these refugees, they no longer had a home. And lying on the layers of carpets in an open-air tent was the closest thing they may have had in terms of safety and security for a very, very long time. We watched from a distance as the Jordanians began the administration of people, recording names, dates of births, and locations. For many of these refugees, they had just completed an absolutely harrowing experience, dodging bullets from the Syrian regime, facing starvation and the ever-present violent extremist organization. So before we started our work, we wanted to make sure they were settled and at least had something to eat.

We had set up a little table outside of our container that was out of sight of the other tents. The goal was to find someone who had an interesting story that could help us gather information, and then bring him over there where we could essentially debrief them in private. We then went about networking, mingling, essentially speed dating through the refugees to try to find someone who could give us the ambiguous information that we were looking for. To our surprise, everyone wanted to talk. They were overly eager to share their stories, to tell us about their former homes and their journey. We quickly realized that we would have to divide our forces and conquer. If someone had information about food, water, or shelter, they would go speak with the civil affairs personnel. If someone had information on the Syrian Regime, they would talk with me and another person. And if it was some other information that we weren't prepared for, we would all take it down and later figure out how to incorporate it into our data during our late-night team meetings.

Toward the end of the first day, we found a young kid who came from the nearby city of Dar'a. I can't remember his name; surely we asked it to be cordial, but we didn't collect it. He was essentially still a teenager, but apparently, he had been fighting in Dar'a for some time. His family was already in the Zaatari refugee camp, and he was going to visit them. That sounded a bit strange because he made it seem like he was going on vacation to see them in the refugee camp; red flags went up immediately. I knew that there was more to this story, so I brought him over to our little work area, which was filled with Wild Tiger energy drinks and cigarettes. Another teammate and I sat with him and talked for about twenty minutes, at which point I offered him a smoke and indulged with him—cigarette diplomacy. That simple act of good faith or show of goodwill opened Pandora's box with this kid, because the next thing I know, he is showing me his cell phone and grainy videos of what looked like him firing a BGM-71 TOW missile.

A BGM-71 TOW missile is a wire-guided anti-tank missile that was one of the many weapons that the US, along with European allies and Middle Eastern partners, had supplied to the FSA beginning in 2012. I asked this young fighter a bit more about his unit, who was in charge, and what their orders were. He began to rattle off a list of names and factions that we had heard through the rumor mill, but it was the first time that we had been able to corroborate with firsthand information. But one name he kept saying was foreign to us, "Da'esh." I wrote it down as "Dash/Dash?" and thanked him for his time. Before we shook hands and he went back to the tent, he asked me where I was from, and I gave him the party line "oh…we're from Canada. Alberta, Canada." I've never been to Alberta, but it seemed like a safe bet.

Then he reached over to me and, as I was wearing a short sleeve shirt, pulled up my sleeve a bit to get a look at my tattoos. A seemingly harmless thing. So, I indulged him and pulled up the shirt, displaying a half-sleeve tattoo decorated in military items: a clipper ship, West Point sabers, and an American flag. He looked at me curiously and gave me a little bit of a crocodile smile as if to say, "I knew it."

Over the next several days, we had numerous encounters like this. Granted they didn't always go according to plan. Sometimes the males stonewalled us, other times they were inconsolable. And while we talked to hundreds of people during our week there, the one common theme or topic that we kept hearing was about this group of foreign fighters, with red beards, that were not part of the FSA but were ransacking cities and towns and instituting Sharia law, largely up north where they had taken over an old fortress in a town called, as I scribbled, "Rocka."

It would later turn out that this group that I called "Dash" from "Rocka" was actually Da'esh from Ar-Raqqah; Da'esh being the Arabic name for the Islamic State of Iraq and the Levant (ISIL) and Ar-Raqqah their de-facto "capital." There's no way any one of us could have known at the time, but the information we were providing back to our unit was one of the first reports about the terrorist group ISIL and put nearly every US intelligence agency in a tailspin to find out where this city called "Rocka" was and who these guys were.

Looking back now and knowing the impact that our little team was having, it's surreal to think that information we were relaying from a small Nokia cell phone in the middle of the Jordanian desert was somehow making it up to and in the Presidential Daily Brief (PDB). And while there are some great anecdotes about this mission and our time spent there, along with some of the most important work I had done to that point, when I flash back to that time in my mind, the only images I see are those of the children.

There were hundreds of them. Innocent faces victimized in a conflict and war that they had nothing to do with—hell, many weren't even alive when it first started. War was all they knew. They were in essence trained in the same TTPs that many military service members are trained in—i.e., seek hardened shelter during IDF attacks—and they had seen things that I can't even fathom seeing at their ages. And while to them I was just a white-faced stranger with shaggy hair and a patchy beard, and I knew that I was there on an explicit and simple mission to gain information about the current OE in Syria, my personal implied task was just as important: to make these kids laugh, play, feel safe, and most importantly, be kids.

When we'd finish with our interviews, or our team needed to take a break from some of the heartbreaking and wrenching stories we were recording, we were always quick to head outside where there was no shortage of wide-eyed kids waiting to talk to the Americans. And our team collectively obliged.

Some of the kids played with us while others stayed sheltered with their family. Some were outgoing and rambunctious, while others were cautious and silent. We'd often play a game of Pictionary with them, where we'd draw an animal or object, and they would guess it in English, or we would try to guess it in Arabic. It always got a lot of laughs, mainly because of my terrible drawings of cats and dogs. Which I admit were pretty bad but given that they were drawn on the back pages of notes about ISIL, AQ, and the Syrian Regime, it was the best I could do.

In the grand scheme of things, for us to entertain those kids for a couple of hours a day was nothing. In our minds, if anything, it allowed their parents who had just traveled hundreds of miles with all their earthly belongings on their backs to get some rest in the big circus-like tent the families were occupying. But for those kids, coming from a war zone and being welcomed to safety by a group of goofy Americans with funny accents, it may have meant the world.

Through our interpreters we'd ask them about their families or favorite activities, always trying not to bring up traumatic things or situations. The older kids would tell us how they couldn't wait to go back to school, and how they wanted to be doctors or engineers like their family members had been. The hope that these kids—victims of war—had for their future was a tragic display of beautiful ignorance.

But that all came crashing down and reality set in when, as we were playing a game with them, a standard civilian plane flew overhead. And instead of watching it fly over in amazement at the marvels of physics and technology, every child at the camp began screaming, crying, and running. It was heart wrenching to watch, and while we had provided some sense of happiness and joy, this was a gut punch back to reality. Their innocence was destroyed, and their future was taken from them, due to no fault of their own. They were and are the real victims of war and are the faces that I vividly remember and voices I will never forget.

Chapter 12

SCARLET LETTERS

I left Jordan in the summer of 2014, having just had one of the most incredible yet indelible experiences of my life, and returned to Fort Bliss, Texas. There was no fanfare when I arrived back in El Paso, no parent there to greet me, hell, my own boss didn't even know that I was back in the US. I guess my arrival back to the states was foreshadowing what was to come.

I had already made the decision that my time in the active-duty military was up. I loved the military, loved the service members—Soldiers, Sailors, Airmen, and Marines—that I served with, and absolutely loved serving my country, but I was ready for the next chapter. Prior to deploying months earlier, I had put all my belongings into storage, and coming back, knowing that I only had a couple months left until the next adventure—chapter—of my life as a civilian, I didn't even bother to move them out into my new apartment. For the next few months, I was going to live rather spartanly with only an air mattress, camping chair, and cast-iron skillet. It was after all temporary, and I was transient.

As I got settled in my new humble abode, lying on my twin-sized, half-deflated air mattress, I had reflections that would turn into thoughts, internal monologues, self-debates about the virtue of my service, the operational impact that I—we—had in the greater scheme of US national security interests, and if I—we—had done anything to actually make the world a better and safer place. More times than not, as I wrestled with these ideas, I was left more disappointed than I had hoped and certainly wanted.

While I loved the military, every day I would question what we were doing and if the seemingly mundane activities, tasks, and operations we did—both at home and abroad—were having an impact on anything. It was a rather foolish notion in hindsight because now knowing what I know, with the experiences I have since gained, I can unequivocally say that we absolutely were making a difference everywhere we went. But the thoughts I had, the disdain that was festering, and frankly the disenfranchisement I was living with, while directed towards the military, was not coming from the military. In fact, they were symptoms of something altogether different.

When a person is under stress, their body produces two hormones: cortisol and adrenaline. These hormones are essentially those that trigger the fight-or-flight response we always hear about. Here's a simple explanation from the Mayo Clinic:

> "Adrenaline increases your heart rate, elevates your blood pressure, and boosts energy supplies. Cortisol, the primary stress hormone, increases sugars (glucose) in the bloodstream, enhances your brain's use of glucose, and increases the availability of substances that repair tissues. Cortisol also curbs functions that would be nonessential or harmful in a fight-or-flight situation. It alters immune system responses and suppresses the digestive system, the reproductive system, and growth processes. This complex natural alarm system also communicates with the brain regions that control mood, motivation, and fear." – *The Mayo Clinic,* July 8, 2021.

The long-term activation of this system due to prolonged stress can have long-term effects on a person's health, including things like sleep problems, anxiety, and depression. The National Institutes of Health (NIH) conducted a study on sixty survivors from the World Trade Center attacks on 9/11 and found that those survivors experiencing a comorbidity of post-traumatic stress disorder (PTSD) and depression had significantly higher levels of cortisol compared to baseline groups with only one symptom or no symptoms at all. So, what does this mean?

After my deployment to Jordan, I knew that something was wrong. I lived on the brink of wanting to get into bar fights with any person who looked at me the wrong way to breaking down crying at the sight of a malnourished child on a public service announcement. I was living in a world of extremes. Extremes that I could not control. I felt hopeless in every sense of the word. I had just come from one of the worst places on earth, bearing witness to some of the worst atrocities of the twenty-first century, but being back in America, it felt like none of that mattered. I felt like an outcast, like I didn't have anyone to talk to or confide in, or anyone who could share my experiences and feelings. I saw no hope, no help, and no future.

I had sleepless nights routinely where I would lie awake wondering if I even mattered. Had I made an impact on anyone or anything? It was a familiar refrain. I pondered whether the world would even know if I were gone. I felt like I was living on an island of loneliness. Ideations of taking my own life permeated my daily thoughts. Visions of driving my Jeep Wrangler off one of the Interstate-10 bridges gave a bit of respite from the pit of despair I was living in.

I never attempted suicide, and I never had a plan to. I've had numerous friends, both from West Point and from the Army, who have succumbed to suicide, so I know that the pains of suicide forever haunt the surviving friends and family. I couldn't do that to my parents. And finally, I made the decision that I wouldn't. I made the decision that I was sick and tired of being sick and tired. The risk of not doing anything was far greater than anything else—namely stigma—that I would face. So, I made a phone call.

Walking into the mental health center at the military facility, I needed every ounce of courage and stubbornness not to just turn around and walk out. There's an unfortunate stigma with mental health in in America—which is slowly getting better—but this is also greatly exacerbated in the military. Granted, the military and senior leaders have gone through great lengths to encourage military service members to seek help, counseling, and assistance, but back in 2014, that just wasn't really the case. Walking into my appointment and checking in at the front desk, and being asked what I was there for, I tried to keep my voice and tenor down as I nearly whispered "mental health" to the young soldier serving as a receptionist. Sitting in the waiting room, I had an unwarranted sense of shame as I endlessly kept scrolling through nonsensical social media updates on my phone until: "Captain DeMarco… this way…"

After several minutes of awkwardly talking about my feelings and doing other random standardized tests, I left the office with a prescription and a diagnosis: PTSD. I then made one of the most difficult phone calls ever. It wasn't difficult in retrospect, but I made it so. Having what felt like the scarlet letter of PTSD, I called my dad.

Upon hanging up the phone, my dad was on the next plane from Florida to Texas. He understood that I was in a bad place, and as much as I wanted to just be alone, I needed him. We spent the next several days eating too much food, watching too much television, and simply just being together. We didn't speak much, and we didn't need to. And most importantly, he understood that he'll never understand what I was going through. And there are no words to explain what that means except to say that sometimes in life it's the little things that matter the most.

Dealing with this new diagnosis was an eye-opening experience. Maybe because I had lost friends to suicide, maybe because I'm just a natural extrovert, or maybe because I'm just someone who has never followed the well-worn path, but I was extremely open with my diagnosis. I had been sinking into the quicksand, but thankfully I was pulled up by a community of friends and family. I was one of the lucky ones. Because not everyone has that communal support structure available, and I knew this. So, in essence, I knew that if I was open with my troubles that maybe, just maybe, I could help someone else who is suffering in silence. And maybe, just maybe, I could be the hand to pull someone out of the quicksand.

Later that summer, I began my transition from active-duty military service, and decided to move to Washington, DC. A place I had always admired and loved since I was a little kid. A place where I spent countless summers exploring the litany of museums and historical locations: "Here is where this happened."

For as bad as my year had been, returning from the deployment, dealing with my own personal struggles and battles, being branded by my condition, it was an exciting time as I began to look at and write the next chapter. I was eager to grow a beard, looking forward to having a new hair style, and curious as to what my daily work attire would be as I'd have to wear a suit and tie versus the same sweaty uniform I wore day in and day out. I packed up my

Jeep Wrangler, hooked up a small U-Haul trailer, and with my dad by my side, drove the nearly thirty-six-hour cross-country trip to the capital of the free world.

Chapter 13

TRANSITIONS

As I got settled in DC, I quickly sought to immerse myself in everything I could. Happy hours with new colleagues, coffee with friends of friends of friends, supporting philanthropic groups and being a "man about town," or at least trying to be. DC is a fascinating city that gets a terrible rap. The history alone provides for more than enough entertainment, but the inner workings of the high society of this swamp also provide for some incredible opportunities, exclusive events, and hilarious people watching.

I tended to find myself in such exclusive events asking myself, "How the hell did I get here?" Or often saying, "I definitely shouldn't be here." I was always comically finding myself in rooms with people, perennially underdressed, with a boy scout smirk, taking every moment in. I met with senators, joined private members-only clubs, got private tours of the Capitol, and even went to the White House Christmas parties. But all of that, or none of that, compared to the friendship I developed with Mr. Doug Coe.

I was introduced to Mr. Coe in 2015 through a network of friends and was invited to meet him at a beautiful estate in Arlington called the Cedars. Pulling up, I could see the Cedars was an immaculate colonial mansion nestled in the rolling hill of a nondescript neighborhood across the Potomac from Georgetown.

There was a carriage house adjacent to the house, which is where, I presumed, I would meet Mr. Coe. Walking in, this time in a suit and tie, I was met by a very lovely secretary who gave me a quick tour and then ushered me into a large meeting room. There, in the corner, was an older and larger man, quietly reading: Mr. Doug Coe.

Doug Coe was an evangelical leader of a group called The Fellowship, which has been portrayed in books and documentaries as a somewhat nefarious organization that controls the strings of governments around the world. It's also often referred to as "The Family." I was fortunate enough to meet Doug, and he in many ways became an advisor and mentor, not just spiritually, but in all things.

We would meet often and talk about life, and more importantly, the life of Jesus. Doug's spiritual philosophy was simple: "Jesus plus nothing." It was an interesting take for me—someone who grew up studying both the Old and New Testaments in Catholic school—but in many ways it resonated with me, and not just because of his charisma, but because of my experiences.

Having just spent nearly a year in an area of the world that many of these stories were written in or about, my faith in some of the Old Testament—specifically the book of Leviticus—well, it was waning. However, the message of Jesus was one that I found to not only believe in but espouse to uphold. The compassion for all, the love of others, and the simplest message of his "Golden Rule"—the ethic of reciprocity—are the most fundamental.

And this was exactly Doug's message as well. I learned through Doug that his ministry, his "family," was solely centered on the Gospels of Matthew, Mark, Luke, and John: the story and life of Jesus Christ. During one meeting with Doug, he handed me a small marble that was painted like the Earth, and a book that was simply titled *Jesus*; it was the four gospels and only those four gospels—"Jesus plus nothing."

Doug and I had a perfectly odd relationship. Maybe he saw himself in me, or maybe I saw myself in him, or maybe we just saw each other as two people doing the best we could with what we have. I'll never know. But I cherished the many times I spent with him whether at big cookouts and picnics at the Cedars or picking him up from his house to go get hamburgers in Annapolis. And, yes, even at his old age, he always requested that we take my Jeep Wrangler.

Sadly, Mr. Coe passed away only a year after we met. He had a profound impact on my life in more ways than one, and I will always value his friendship. There's a lot that could be and has been said about his life. Things that I only learned after his passing, but in retrospect make one of our interactions much more notable.

One day when I was sitting with him at the Cedars, as he told me of his work in Africa, he looked at me with a very stark face and asked me, "Do you have any enemies?" That was a very strange question for me. Of course, I had faced enemies of the United States overseas, but he was asking me if I had any personal enemies. I fumbled for an answer, and thankfully realized it was rhetorical, as he then began to tell me of his. The list was long and distinguished, but for Doug, and based on what I learned and observed from him, none of that mattered. If he was doing what he believed was the right thing, then he would continue his life's work.

During those times, and as I continued to struggle with my own battles and demons, Mr. Coe never once judged me. He simply accepted me for me—faults and all—and would always say that we were brothers in this journey called life, that we are all in this thing together, and kindness to one another is the strongest currency we have with the greatest return.

Shortly after Mr. Coe passed away, I received other terrible news. On March 8, 2016, I was leaving the local gym in DC's posh Navy Yard neighborhood when I got a text from a former teammate of mine at West Point. Mike Lemming, who like me had just left the army and was now living in Nashville, simply wrote "call me." That's always the worst text to receive, second only to "we need to talk," so given that I called him and almost collapsed with the news.

Taylor Force, one of my best friends, the same Taylor whom I had spent countless days and nights with in Iraq, the guy who had always had my back, and the same guy who would drag me to Austin's only country line dancing bar nearly every weekend, was killed earlier that day in Jaffa, Israel. There wasn't any more information than that, but word was spreading and fast.

In the following hours, I learned that Taylor was on a study abroad trip with his graduate school class from Vanderbilt, where he was studying to earn a Master of Business Administration degree. They were on the boardwalk in Jaffa, and a Palestinian terrorist had gone on a rampage and stabbed several people. And it was there, on the boardwalk, that Taylor was killed. It was a senseless act of terrorism that has no justification and provides no closure.

In the days after, Israel hosted several events to honor Taylor and even sent a delegation to attend the funeral. Several national news outlets ran stories about Taylor, and I was contacted numerous times by reporters about it. It was my first time dealing with the press so I wasn't too sure how to respond. I gave a few responses to questions from a couple of people, thinking that the respective outlets they worked for were developing a story about Taylor. Benny Johnson, the now firebrand media personality, was one of them. I didn't know the guy but saw that he had somehow posted on Twitter a couple of photos of Taylor and me, and then the reality set in. I should have known better—I was after all living in DC—but the death of Taylor was an absolute horrific tragedy, and it was now being used as political fodder.

I couldn't make the funeral—a regret I still live with—but watched the live stream of it from the church in Texas. Seeing many of my friends, classmates, former brothers and sisters in arms all together for this tragedy was heartbreaking. I can't speak for everyone certainly, but at funerals we are always told to honor and celebrate the life that the dearly departed had, but this just felt different. While Taylor had done so much for so many people, we all knew he was just getting started.

There was a sense of denial that we all had, that no way did this happen to Taylor. It was unbelievable, until we came to terms with having to believe it. Our friend groups would often text one another funny stories or try to find funny photos to remind ourselves of the good times with Taylor. But during this grieving process, we managed to find out one thing that Taylor did that he rarely told anyone about, which truly shows his character and, well, is the perfect testament to his life.

After coming back from Iraq, Taylor remained in contact with our interpreters and would check in on them from time to time—just like he did with all his friends. Fully knowing the precariousness of the situation in Iraq and the very likelihood of the security situation deteriorating quickly, Taylor began the process to sponsor our interpreter and his family under the Special Immigrant Visa (SIV) program to be able to come to the United States and eventually become American citizens. While this may seem like a small gesture, for those who have worked with or served American military forces during our campaigns in the

Middle East, offering to sponsor someone for the arduous SIV process is one of the most special and important things a person can do for a foreign ally or partner. And Taylor had done that, and never even told any of us. That was the kind of guy he was.

In the weeks following the funeral, I had a special bracelet made to honor Taylor. The kind that military service members and veterans wear to honor the lives and legacies of the fallen. It says on it, "Taylor Allen Force," and underneath has the inscription "Be thou at peace," a line from the West Point alma matter. But it's the preceding line from our alma matter that suits this bracelet and his life better, and that is "May it be said, well done."

Chapter 14

ECHOES AND WHISPERS

On August 12, 2017, I was sitting at a hotel bar in downtown Munich, Germany. I was in town for a graduate school event in Frankfurt but arrived a couple of days early to go do a little exploring via the autobahn, the famed German highway system with no speed limits. And, yes, the kid who barely graduated high school decided to go to, or more accurately was graciously and generously accepted into, Georgetown University's graduate programs at the Walsh School of Foreign Service and McDonough Business School; crazy how things sometimes turn out.

I was fighting the good fight to beat jet lag over a couple of pilsners with some older German gentlemen seated next to me. I think they were from the surrounding area, but my knowledge of German geography at that point was minimal. Through their thick German accents, seemingly all they wanted to talk about was politics, American politics. As we laughed about the various caricatures in modern American society—it was after the 2016 election featuring Donald Trump and Hillary Clinton—I couldn't help but notice a headline run across the bottom screen of CNN International. It was about a protest of some sort back in the US, which wasn't all too uncommon those days, but something had happened. The headline disappeared before I could get more information, but then the screen interrupted their programming with a "Breaking News" banner and cut over to the scene. My conversation with the Germans immediately stopped, and the three of us watched in what went from silent curiosity to horrified terror.

The images on the screen were filled with Nazi swastikas and Confederate battle flags, and grown men clad in full battle gear assaulting people who I presumed were counter protestors. And then the video footage of a car plowing through a crowd aired. I sat there in silence as the footage replayed people flying over the hood of the vehicle, and then the footage of the aftermath and carnage that both the weaponized vehicle and the entire protest left. It was surreal, even from thousands of miles away.

The Unite the Right protest in Charlottesville, Virginia, was a horrific stain on our country. It not only brought out the worst of American society or the darkest of American sins but allowed these people—these "patriots"—to celebrate them proudly and openly through weaponized speech, which turned to violence and resulted in the death of thirty-two-year-old Heather Heyer.

Looking at my new German friends, I felt sickened, embarrassed, and ashamed. Germans have a contentious time dealing with their own history. The association of Germany with the Nazi party is a point to which almost all Germans wish they could forget but believe they have a responsibility to remember. And while anything related to the Nazis is outlawed—logos, flags, even the Nazi salute—underground far right movements have begun to adopt the American Civil War era Confederate battle flag as their new de facto fascist standard.

Sitting there on the bar stool, I quickly realized that I wasn't the only one feeling this way either. I could see in my newfound German friends' eyes the pain that these images brought out. Because, like for me, seeing these images harkened back to the deepest darkest original sins of our beloved countries. The irony wasn't lost either that I was watching this all unfold in the birthplace of the Nazi party.

Flying back to the states a week later, I was still in this fog as to what was going on in America. Granted I had just spent the week holed up in classes and seminars, so I was pretty burned out from the hundreds of pages of readings, but on the flight back from Frankfurt to Washington, DC, I began playing catch up a bit on everything that had happened since the horrible events in Charlottesville. And that's when I first heard it.

On August 15, 2017, while answering media questions from the lobby of Trump Tower in New York, President Donald Trump made the following statement: "...you had some very bad people in that group. But you also had people that were very fine people, on both sides." That quote cut like a knife, and only three days after the act of domestic terrorism—as that's what it was—the commander in chief, the president of the United States, effectively gave a pass to those white supremacists, neo-Nazis, Confederate sympathizers, ultra-right-wing groups, and the scores of other playground-named groups of men playing army who were not only in Charlottesville that day, but openly espoused those beliefs across America.

Later that fall, with the images of Charlottesville and the follow-on rhetoric still permeating the air, I was invited to a Veterans Day event in New York City hosted by the organization Iraq and Afghanistan Veterans of America (IAVA). It was a rather traditional fundraising gala with comedian Stephen Colbert hosting and a litany of special guests including both veterans and celebrities. During the event, then Secretary of Veterans Affairs Robert McDonald, who goes simply by Bob, also a West Point graduate, said something that I've heard countless times before, but for some reason it struck a chord with me that evening: "We stand on the shoulders of the giants that have come before us."

It's a powerful statement, and one that in that moment in that gala nearly brought a tear to my eye. I thought about the perfectly aligned rows of headstones at Arlington National Cemetery, where so many have given the last full measure of devotion for this country. I thought about my grandfathers who themselves sacrificed so much for this American experiment. And finally, I remembered how many families continue to endure the loss of a loved one in combat—Gold Star families—and how they deserve so much more than this. For generations, American service men and service women have fought and died on distant shores and at home for this idea of America. Yet, here we were, in a politically corrosive and toxic environment. It didn't happen overnight, and it didn't happen with the election of one person or one party.

On the train back home the next day, that refrain kept echoing in my head. Sitting alone on the nearly empty Amtrak train from NYC to DC, passing through cities and towns where the idea of America was founded and where American independence was earned, the echoes became louder.

I truly believe that God does have a plan for all of us, and I also believe that sometimes we miss the signs that He gives us. Some might call it destiny, providence, or just a gut instinct, but as I sat there, I couldn't help but think about the historical context of our current domestic environment. How did it get so bad? Well, there's certainly a long and dated list of grievances that everyone could point to, but at that exact moment, I realized that the fundamental reason why is because we Americans don't look at each other as brothers and sisters under the same flag. George Washington warned us of this during his 1796 farewell address by stating that partisanship "serves always to distract the public councils and enfeeble the public administration. It agitates the community with ill-founded jealousies and false alarms, kindles the animosity of one part against another, foments occasionally riot and insurrection."

We needed leadership to right this ship, and we needed it now. Maybe purely coincidence, or maybe something else, but as the train passed through Philadelphia—where our country was founded—those same echoes that were reverberating were now whispers. Were they instructions? Were they orders? Or was it simply a figment of my imagination? I then grabbed my phone and typed the follow phrase into the Google search bar: "how to run for Congress."

Chapter 15

THE GREATER FOOL

U p to that point I had been in the process of moving to Baltimore, where I was born, and was looking at starting a new business and a new chapter. Baltimore is a historic city in the story of America that unfortunately has failed to keep up with the opportunities of the twenty-first century and deal with the challenges of a swiftly changing economy. Living in historic Fells Point was, for a history nerd, nearly a dream come true. But for all practicality, and with the rampant crime, it was often a nightmare. Baltimore was a city that was failed by its leaders, such as disgraced former and convicted felon Mayor Catherine Pugh.

Living in Fells Point, I was a resident of the Maryland 3rd Congressional District. It is, by far, the most gerrymandered district in this history of gerrymandering. Looking like a pterodactyl in a Rorschach test, the district winds its way from Baltimore to Annapolis, then down south to the suburbs of Washington, DC. Passing through four counties, the design of the district is a result of decades of red lining and political jockeying from both Democrats and Republicans alike.

This district seat at that point was held by Representative John Sarbanes, a legacy political figure whose father, Paul, served as a senator in the United States Congress from 1977 to 2007. John, from what I gather, was and still is a nice guy. I briefly met him once in passing, but that was it. However, at this point both in my life and in what I viewed as the direness of our American crisis, we could no longer afford to sit idly by or to simply wait and see how things played out.

There's an old African proverb that says, "If there's no enemy inside, the enemy outside can do us no harm." But I believed that our country was unfortunately getting ever nearer to an inflection point where the enemy within was more dangerous than the external threats we faced. And we needed a new generation of leaders to tackle those problems, take on the challenges, and seize the opportunities.

There was only one problem: I had never worked in or around politics or politicians, or even campaigns, for that matter. I had worked as a legislative liaison in the Pentagon for a couple of months when I joined the National Guard, but that work was more about getting people coffee and bagels than really doing any substantial work on Capitol Hill. I had a handful of friends that had done this work who began advising me on what this would look like, how a campaign operates, and what to be prepared for if I went down this path. Most of all, the idea of taking on an institutional Democrat such as Sarbanes in a primary challenge was not only an uphill battle but viewed as an impractical adventure reminiscent more of Don Quixote than Thomas Jefferson.

Looking through thousands of pages of studies, census data, and voter information files, I began to formulate a plan akin to how to build this campaign out. Sitting down to map this all out—and yes, I was using maps—the campaign ended up looking more like a military operation than a political campaign. I had data points for how many voters were in various sections and sectors of the district, a multitude of data points for how many of them were veterans, and even the granularity of how many voted or didn't vote in previous primary elections. I even had the names, numbers, and email addresses of all the registered voters in the district. It was the making of what I thought was going to be the most brilliant information operation campaign ever—a military approach to a political campaign—yet also slightly disconcerting.

I had built out this plan from the ground up but still hadn't fully decided if this was going to happen. I mean, there were numerous variables still out there that I needed to gauge. Thankfully, I didn't have a family that I had to factor into this decision, but stepping into the political arena in the charged environment of 2020 would essentially change everything for me. I had to be ready, willing, and able to meet that head on, and be able to go "all in," poker parlance for putting all my chips in on one hand. I've never been a big gambler, but if I were to ever hedge my bets, to put my money into or on anything, it would be on me and on my name.

So in December of 2017, after seeking advice and counsel, weighing the pros and cons, and understanding the gravity and potential second- and third-order effects, I walked into the Maryland State Board of Elections, signed a couple of papers, and that was it. I was now officially a congressional candidate for Maryland's Third Congressional District. And now the clock was ticking. The primary Election Day was set for June 26, 2018, and it was time to get to work.

What Google doesn't tell you when you search "how to run for Congress" is that the real challenge of politics in the twenty-first century is "name recognition," nor does it explain the absolute emotional rollercoaster that a campaign can and will be. You can have the most monumental and incredible program or legislation in the history of public policy, but none of that matters if no one knows who you are. I was never really involved in politics and had never really been involved in community organizing. Yet while I had some rough legislative experience I gained from my military assignment on Capitol Hill, and I understood the premise of "how a bill becomes a law," what I certainly didn't understand or have any experience in is how a person "actually" becomes a Congressional member. And frankly, it was an eye-opening experience to say the least.

If you've ever met a candidate for office, you must know that the two limiting factors that their entire life revolves around are money and time. And if there was one common thread across my life it was that I had little of both factors. I didn't come from a family with money, and the little money I did have was the result of overworking myself in two or three jobs while trying to maintain some semblance of sanity. So being spread thin as it was, I knew that I would have to approach this campaign in an unconventional manner. However, I had one piece of knowledge that I believed would help bridge the resource gap of my campaign: an understanding of insurgency and counterinsurgency operations.

During my deployments, I had been put into austere positions in nonpermissive environments and had to adapt. Any service member who deployed during the Global War on Terror (GWOT) or Overseas Contingency Operations (OCO) periods understands this. When I was a young lieutenant before I was deployed to Iraq, I had a binder of materials that I brought with me that served as foundational knowledge for our operations. In that binder was an article by Australian author, strategist, and counterinsurgency expert, David Kilcullen, who served as a counterterrorism coordinator for the Department of State and advised General David Petraeus during the Iraq surge of 2006 to 2007. His article, "Twenty-Eight Articles: Fundamentals of Company-Level Counterinsurgency," was a practical guide that I then used as the basis for my "tactical campaign plan."

When I began building my team of volunteers, champions, and interns, I sent everyone this article and let them know that our campaign was going to be one that goes against the big money political system. We were going to operate as if we were conducting a counterinsurgency campaign against a much larger field of competitors. David Kilcullen's piece summed up my idea perfectly: "This is a competition with the insurgent for the right and the ability to win the hearts, minds, and acquiescence of the population." We'll never outraise the incumbent or other candidates, but if we operated light, fast, and hard—as Kilcullen prescribes—we could essentially win the primary and the day. It was a gamble. A risky maneuver, and a fool-hearted decision.

There's an unfortunate reality in twenty-first century America, and that is while we believe that American democracy centers around the fundamental ideas of our founders, the truth is that it really revolves around money. If you've ever signed up to support a candidate, whether for the local school board or for the highest office in the land, you've submitted your personal information, which is then used to solicit donations. Then, as a candidate, I could access your information and directly contact you to solicit support—which really means money—to fund things such as advertisements or to pay consultants and staff. I hated it. And furthermore, as I brought on people or met with organizations that wanted to work with my campaign or provide an endorsement, the first question they would always ask was "How much money have you raised?" To which I would proudly respond, "I'm not focused on that, I'm spending my time pounding the ground and knocking on doors." A response that showed the perfect blend of young confidence, misdirected arrogance, and indignant ignorance.

Foolish pride is a dangerous thing. It's why Lord Cornwallis was defeated at the Battle of Cowpens in 1781, why Napoleon invaded Russia in the middle of winter in 1812, and why my campaign was doomed from the start.

There's a term that is used in politics called "viability." A political candidate earns this term through the quarterly financial disclosures they make that show how much money they have raised. And unfortunately, this is the barometer that proves the viability of a candidate to major news outlets, special interest groups, political action committees, and the rest of the political class of America. So, while I was proud that I wasn't spending my nights calling potential voters, friends, and family for money, I was never going to be seen as a real candidate. And that all came to a head one night at a college meet and greet with prospective candidates, voters, supporters, and students.

I was at the University of Maryland, Baltimore County for a gubernatorial candidate forum that would also include a meet and greet for all candidates on the upcoming primary ballot. I arrived, solo, and quietly faded into the back of the room as several gubernatorial candidates were on stage giving their elevator pitches and stump speeches. After the formalities were over, I began mixing and mingling with those in attendance.

When talking with several students who, I presume, were political science majors, I remember one of them asked me how much money I raised. I explained that my campaign was one of ideas and not money, to which this astute student responded, "So… are you running just to run?" I was pissed.

How dare this kid question me like that. I knew I was an outsider running a dark horse campaign. I knew I was a long shot and underdog from the get-go. But I had put everything I had into this "mission." And to be judged by someone as a not-serious-not-real-candidate, or the implication that I was simply an imposter, deeply cut me to my core. And the worst part was, deep down inside, I knew that kid was probably right.

Was I a fraud? Was I really doing things for the right reason? I began to feel like I was stuck living in a glass house, screaming at the top of my lungs, watching the world go by as no one paid any attention to me. The impostor syndrome I began to feel weighed heavily on me. I questioned everything after that. Whenever I am doing anything, I often challenge myself to answer two introspective questions: "Am I doing things right?" and "Am I doing the right things?" And while I jumped into this campaign to help make a difference and have a positive impact, the reality was that I knew it was a lost cause from the get-go. The light of my campaign quickly flickered and fluttered. It was a sinking ship, and I was at the helm. That was until February 14, 2018.

On February 14, 2018, reports came out of an active shooter—and this is abhorrent to say—but at first it was just another school shooting. But then I learned that it was at Marjory Stoneman Douglas High School in Parkland, Florida. Having grown up in South Florida, I immediately knew where this was, as it was close to the park where I grew up playing baseball as a little kid.

As the details emerged about the shooting, about the actions that were or weren't taken, and most importantly the horrific scale of this tragedy, I felt a sickening feeling. The same feelings that I hadn't felt since 9/11. Feelings of sorrow, anger, and hopelessness. But, unlike after 9/11, this time I was in a different position, place, and time. This time I could actually do something. Even though I had a relatively small microphone as a political candidate—although seen as an outsider, outcast, and imposter—I knew that I could at least start the conversation to address changes needed or how to prevent the next school mass shooting. Because unless action was taken and this epidemic was addressed, there would—and this once again sickens me to say—be another.

I then began rummaging through the 1994 Public Safety and Recreational Firearms Use Protection Act and the provisions that the bill had and, more importantly, the criticisms that it drew. This Clinton-era act is commonly known as the "Assault Weapons Ban," which expired in 2004. I thought that with my military experience, my understanding of the legislative process, and more importantly, my belief in the rule of law and adherence to the United States Constitution, I could at least help push some and drive the conversation on this topic.

Around the same time as I was working on drafting this type of plan or program, the kids from Parkland began their own outreach efforts under the banner of "March For Our Lives." This was essentially a grassroots movement that organically sprung up chapters across the United States in what was a compelling and inspiring display of democracy in action. Then in March, the students from Marjory Stoneman Douglas along with tens of thousands of students and supporters held the March For Our Lives rally in Washington, DC.

I came down to support the seemingly hundreds of thousands of students who put this on. Albeit the circumstances for the event were terrible, seeing these kids—the future of America—stand up to authority and stand for their own rights was inspirational. However, seeing how many of them were ostracized in the media world for this was despicable, specifically through some of the extreme conservative right-wing channels. These kids, these survivors, had and have every right to be heard by those in authority positions, and to try to berate and assassinate the character of these kids—by adults, mind you—was pathetic.

But the one interesting thing that I took away from the event came in speaking with several of the survivors from the latest shooting in Parkland was that they were unapologetically demanding action. And while they appreciated my words of sympathy and support, they were almost confrontational in saying, "What are you going to do about it?" Their conviction was inspiring and a realization that those students not only demanded but deserved action.

A couple of days later, I was back at a candidate event at the University of Maryland, Baltimore County where I had a featured speaking role. The room was filled with students and "politicos"— an interesting dynamic to say the least.

I knew that whatever I said in this canned stump speech would essentially fall on deaf ears as many of the people in this event were already volunteering with or had supported another candidate. Knowing this, and with one of my friends in tow, I asked him what he thought I should say. I had gotten my stump speech nearly memorized; it touched on every piece of social impact–focused legislation I was aimed at working on, from paid family medical leave, to infrastructure, to foreign affairs, but it just didn't feel like it was the right time or place for another stump speech. So, we decided I should wing it, go off script, and speak my thoughts and share a piece of my mind and heart.

I told the group about my recent experiences with the students and survivors from Parkland. How their movement should and must serve as a call to action. We can't afford to sit idly by as the divisions of America continue to tear us apart at the seams. Knowing that this was likely the only time I'd ever address this concentrated group of young college students, I challenged them.

In today's world, now more than ever, it is too easy to fall into the trap of quick slights, vitriolic comments, and ad hominem attacks. Social media has degraded societal norms to the point that we view each other not as people, but as opportunities for us to build our vanity and stroke egos at the expense of others. Civil discourse of generations past ceases to exist, and because of that we fail to appreciate or even acknowledge the merits of someone else's viewpoint. As Americans our commonalities far outweigh our differences, and we need to realize that if we continue to view each other as enemies versus fellow countrymen and women, we will continue down this long road to ruin.

Walking away from that event, which included several senior members of the Maryland Democrat Party who were and are none too happy with me for trying to buck the system, I knew our campaign, our quest, was nearly over. It's hard as a candidate, or even just as a person, to squarely stare into the eyes of defeat and not want to simply end the nightmare by quitting. But much to the chagrin of nearly everyone, and with the advice and support of my mom, I still felt that I could affect some positive change. So, while conventional wisdom would have been to drop out, I "Charlie Miked," and didn't quit.

A week or so later, I contacted two high school students who were involved with and started up their local affiliated March For Our Lives chapters in Annapolis and Baltimore. Initially, I just wanted to congratulate them on their efforts to build awareness and thank them for all they had done. However, I was quickly taken aback by the response.

As a current candidate, they didn't want my thanks, my thoughts, or my prayers; they wanted me to do something. Actually, more importantly, they wanted me to help them do something. To this point, candidate forums were few and far between. My opponent in the race had not attended one, and I had no opportunity to debate him on substantive issues. And while I was resigned to the idea that this entire campaign was a virtual sinking ship, maybe I could help these students host their own forum.

After meeting with the students several times, I decided to help them facilitate a candidate forum to ask tough questions of elected officials and candidates about their plans to secure schools, protect children's lives, and put a tourniquet on the flowing wounds of gun violence in the country. I explained to the students that this would be their event, and I wanted no part in the planning, but I could provide the logistics to support it for them along with the connections to other officials and candidates to attend. The importance of being heard and felt seen should never be discounted, especially by leaders.

They contacted every state and federal elected official and candidate that had a jurisdiction touching Baltimore City and Annapolis to invite them to this open forum. The students' idea was to have an open round table where everyone could share information, insights, and ideas. And most importantly, the candidates could engage directly with the students and vice versa. Out of all the invitations that were sent out by the students, much to my dismay, only a handful of candidates showed up. And then it hit me, this is politics.

To me this was an opportunity to empower the next and future generation to be heard. Was this small forum of nearly a dozen people going to fix this epidemic? Absolutely not. But if this could move the needle even a fraction of a tick mark and inspire future generations to not only pay attention to but engage in the political process, then maybe this will yield some long-term positive impact and, dare I say, "change."

But to others—namely politicos—this was an opportunistic stunt. To some this entire forum led by the students was my way of capitalizing on a tragic situation and hijacking a good cause that was meant to raise awareness and drive change for future generations. That's how cynical our politics have become. It was at that point, that exact moment, that I had a self-realization: I was done. I wanted no part in this shitshow.

I had put myself out there. I had sacrificed a career, relationships, nearly everything, to try to make a positive impact. And all I got was to see the strings inside the political puppet show...and what was an inevitable ass kicking at the polls. But just as I was at my breaking point, right when I was about to close shop on our small campaign office, I sat alone in my one-bedroom apartment in Fells Point, hovering over hundreds of pages of voter contact lists and boxes of unsent postcards spread out across my dining room table. I poured some bourbon and had a moment of true self-reflection. What was I doing? Who was I? And where do I go from here?

Leaning over, I reached to the bottom of my bookcase and pulled out my old West Point yearbook from 2009, called "The Howitzer." Flipping through the pages, I traveled back in time to being a bright-eyed Cadet, eager to take on the world. Where my days were spent learning the lessons of our forebears and nights toasting to future adventures with my soon to be brothers and sisters in arms. The world was my oyster. And now, here I was beaten down, exhausted, almost broke, and nearly broken. But just as I was about to call it a night, I flipped to my own Cadet photo. Staring on the page, it was like looking into a mirror. I could see myself and remember those days, the smile and energy that I had. How things had changed. My face had become a map of the world in the years following, and the bags under my eyes only tell half the story. I thought to myself, what would I say to that young twenty-two-year-old Cadet if I could go back in time. What lessons would I teach him? What would I warn him about? And what advice would I give him? Would I tell him to follow his head or his heart? To take the conventional routes of life or to, as Mark Twain said, "...throw off the bowlines. Sail away from the safe harbor. Catch the trade winds…"

In a moment of pure irony, as I was at one of my lowest points, it was that same kid staring back who gave me advice, and a kick in the ass, instead. Because written underneath the photo of the young Cadet I used to be in my full-dress jacket were the words: "Aim high and never quit."

The next several weeks leading up to Election Day, I continued the mission: "Charlie Mike." I continued to try to gain as much traction, gain as much support, and raise as much awareness as I could, but the inevitable was drawing ever closer. On the night of the primary, I was dejected to the point that I didn't even host an event. So, as I sat in my apartment, endlessly refreshing the *New York Times* database as the votes came in, it became clear: I didn't just get beat. I got beat, bad. And the check mark declaring the opponent the winner was the final nail in my short-lived political career.

Losing sucks. It never gets and should never get easier. When you lose in a team sport, you don't personally lose; it's the team. And as no person is bigger than the team, while it still sucks, there's a veil that guards against taking it too personally. But this loss was different. Because it was my name. It was me on the ballot, not my team. It was my name that will forever be the long shot candidate who proved the bookies right and was trounced. And with that came a level of shame and another scarlet letter. Losing in an election is a terrible feeling. But the only worse feeling would have been quitting.

There's a great quote from one of my favorite Aaron Sorkin shows, *The Newsroom*, where the protagonist Will McAvoy, played by Jeff Daniels, has an absolute disastrous hit piece written about him in *New York* Magazine. The title of this fictional article was "The Greater Fool." With his confidence shot and seemingly his entire world flipped upside down by this, one of his colleagues, a brilliant economist named Sloan Sabbith—played by Olivia Munn—gives him a rousing speech near the very end of the season one finale:

> "The greater fool is actually an economic term. It's a patsy. For the rest of us to profit, we need a greater fool—someone who will buy long and sell short. Most people spend their life trying not to be the greater fool; we toss him the hot potato; we dive for his seat when the music stops. The greater fool is someone with the perfect blend of self-delusion and ego to think that he can succeed where others have failed. This whole country was made by greater fools." – *The Newsroom*, Aaron Sorkin

Am I a greater fool? Maybe. Am I someone with the perfect blend of self-delusion and ego? Well, that's not for me to decide. But what I can say is that while I lost terribly, in a race that I probably had absolutely no reason to run, with my confidence, personal life, and professional career absolutely shattered, looking back now I can finally hold my head up high. Because I ran the race, fought the good fight, I aimed high and didn't quit.

Chapter 16

BROKEN & BROKE

After the summer primary election in 2018, I was not only spiritually broken, but by this time also financially broke. I had put everything I had into this election, up to and including much of my small savings. I was a laughingstock. It was my peak imposter syndrome moment. My name will forever be known as the failed candidate from Maryland's 3ʳᵈ Congressional District. And while I was able to jokingly laugh at myself to my friends, my self-deprecating humor was like putting lipstick on a pig. It did nothing to ease the emotional toll that this loss took.

To make matters worse, I was dead broke. I had left my lucrative job as a corporate consultant and had spent much of my own personal savings on chasing this pipe dream. And now, out of work and running on fumes, I had a very short runway to get back in the air. Moving back to Washington, DC, hopeful that I could find some work given my military experience, I found a tiny studio with a Murphy bed that folded out of the wall. I could essentially scramble eggs with one foot in the shower while watching the television on the cardboard box in the living room—that small. It would have to do.

I knew that I had only two months' worth of money left, and after that, I had some tough decisions to make. What would I do? Would I move in with my parents? Could I crash on someone's couch? There was a lot of uncertainty and each day that passed was one day closer to an even bigger failure.

Well, those two months came and went. There were many nights where I had to look at my dog, George, and decide who was going to eat that night; I'm proud to say that George never went hungry. I was at absolute rock bottom, and there was not a solution at hand or a visible way out. And worse, it was all my fault. There was no one to blame, no excuse to make, and no life raft coming. I was stranded at sea and the waves were swelling.

I had gambled on myself and made a bad bet with the odds stacked against me. As Rudyard Kipling wrote in my favorite poem "*If*," I made a "heap of all of [my] winnings and risked it on one turn of pitch-and-toss…" But the one silver lining in being at rock bottom is that there is no where else to go but up. If you can look up, you can get up.

I was extremely fortunate to be able to reach out to my connections and secure a position back on active-duty military orders. This would not only alleviate the financial concerns but also put me back in a position where I was a part of something again—to give me back the community I so needed and the purpose I was salivating for. The isolation I felt from my political campaign was one of the worst second or third order effects and aspects of my fool's errand. So, as I got my feet back underneath me and began to pick myself up from the proverbial mat, I was excited for this new opportunity—and to be able to have a steady and regular income—but I also had a new challenge and potential problem ahead.

The military is and forever will be nonpartisan, which is one of the most important attributes of our armed forces, along with the civilian control. Externally, these principles are neutral so that the American public can have good faith and trust in the military.

And internally, it's absolutely critical for good order and discipline.

Which is why, when I went on my new assignment to the United States European Command (EUCOM), located in Stuttgart, Germany, I tried my best to keep my secret. This secret that in a not too far away past—five months to be exact—I was in fact a congressional candidate. I did my best to shut down my campaign website and scrub any mention of politics from my social media accounts in the event that one of my new bosses, colleagues, or soldiers would find them. But even a cursory search of my name on Google will pop up with the seemingly damning information and more scarlet letters.

This was my fresh start. It was a massive reset for me to not only get back on my feet, but really to reflect on who I was, what I had accomplished—or not—and where I wanted to go in my life. In life we don't get many opportunities to do this, and while I was working a crazy schedule across crazy hours, trading in my blue suit and lapel pin for the army's combat uniform, I wasn't going to let this opportunity go to waste. So, while I was serving as an executive officer (XO) in EUCOM's joint operational center (JOC), coordinating strategic-level information and operations across the fifty-one countries in EUCOM's AO with every three-letter agency in the US Government, it was ironically also a time for quiet introspection and self-reflection.

Looking back, I wish I had journaled, wrote more notes, blogged, or just annotated situations and my feelings on them. I think as people in a twenty-first century global economy, rushing to the next deal and racing to whatever finish line we have, we fail to sit back and take everything in, to be present, and to reflect on what has been and is to come. My time at EUCOM was just that.

During this period, I really began to learn about myself. Not the name on a résumé, not the biography of the political candidate, and certainly not the person in Google search results, but me. I often found myself relitigating decisions I made and courses of action I took, not focusing on the what but the why. Why did I make those decisions? Was the result all that I hoped for? One of my best friends and Army Football teammate Tom Dyrenforth, who was a firstie while I was a plebe, gave me some incredible advice that I carry to this day. Often at West Point I wanted to leave, I wanted to quit. I wanted to get out of there so fast and go live the life that my friends and other peers were living back in Florida. And every time I'd be down, which was often as a plebe, Tom would always say, "Don't give up what you want most for what you want now." And once again, he was right.

For the past several years, I had been chasing other people's dreams. I had been aiming for other people's goals and trying to live other's people's lives. Sure, I had some great learning experiences—the kind that come with dismal failure—but in doing so I had also sunken to a level of unhappiness that made it hard to even see myself in a mirror. Sure, my life looked great externally, I had mastered the art of telling the good news story, snapping the right photo, and getting closer enough to the nexus of power to look like I belonged, but it was all a façade, it was all bullshit. I was living a life that wasn't mine to be lived. And I was going to fix that.

While in Europe, I really got to know myself. Traveling across foreign countries alone will do that for you. Okay, I take that back. I wasn't alone; George was always with me. Coffee on a mountainside, a beer on a hiking trail, and cheese fondue in the Alps were some of the happiest moments of my life. It was the simplest of pleasures, yet it felt as if I were experiencing everything for the first time.

The train from Stuttgart to Paris is a quick three-hour nonstop trip. And while George and I traveled to nearly every country in Western and Central Europe, I always found myself returning to the "City of Light."

Pulling into the train station, Gare de L'est, felt like traveling back in time to the 1920s and I was jaunting around with Ernest Hemingway and F. Scott Fitzgerald, like I was living a chapter from *A Moveable Feast*, Hemingway's memoir of his time in Paris.

Thomas Jefferson famously said, "A walk about Paris will provide lessons in history, beauty, and in the point of life." And I couldn't agree more. Parisians tend to get a bad rap, in my opinion, especially from us "Yankees." But in my experiences, showing appreciation for Parisian culture and making even the most elementary attempt at assimilation can hopefully break down those thick barricades—French Revolution pun intended.

In the spring of 2019, I decided to run the Paris Marathon. It wasn't my first and certainly wouldn't be my last. I began running marathons when I left active duty, with the ambitious goal of running one marathon a year. I'm not an avid runner and as such wouldn't really, how do you say, train for them? I had my marathon preparation down to a terrible science.

First, maybe incorporate twenty minutes of cardiovascular training to your standard lifting routines in the few weeks leading up to the marathon. Second, the day before the race, "carbo-load," and get absolutely hammered drunk. The kind of drunk that you order enough generic delivery pizza that could feed a Roman feast. And then third, simply show up.

The beauty of this regimen is that by the time you sober up enough to realize you're running a marathon, you're nearly halfway through it. And by this point, you might as well just keep going and finish it because you must get back to where you started anyway, assuming the start and finish line are in the same location. It had worked for nearly a dozen marathons before, so, like a science, it would certainly work again. What I didn't factor in this time was that not only was I older, but I had also pulled my hamstring playing soccer a couple of weeks before.

So, there I was, nearly at the eighteen-mile marker, and I felt something I hadn't felt in a long time. The rush of warm blood, the tension of a cramped muscle, and the pop of the muscle as it for all intents and purposes tore. This was the same sound and feeling I had my junior year at West Point, when in the second game of the season against Wake Forest, I went out for a field goal, and right as I kicked the ball, I tore my groin—however, the kick was still good.

When this happened, I immediately stopped running and limped over to the side. Dejected and disappointed, I figured my race was over. I went there and ran by myself, so there was no cheer squad waiting for me at the finish line. So, no one would have noticed if I didn't finish or stopped running. Now at this point, visibly wobbling, I managed to get to one of the port-a-potties lining the Seine River in front of the Eiffel Tower. I went in, relieved myself, and then began the arduous process of unpinning the bib from my shirt. One by one, my hands shaking from just running nearly three-fourths of a marathon, I began removing the pins to take off the random number I was wearing with my name above it. I decided that I would fold up the bib and hide it, and then slip out from the toilet stall and find a way back to my lonely little hotel room somewhere in the heart of Paris. I had gone nearly my entire life without quitting something. But as I grabbed the bib and began the process of hiding it under my shirt, I took one last look at it and saw my last name, "DeMarco," written at the top. I had been through proverbial hell and back, weathered every storm, faced every challenge head on, and while I'd taken my fair share of bad beats and black eyes, I never once quit. And this, this stupid little run, and my stupid little hamstring, this was finally my kryptonite?

About an hour later, at a snail's pace, I crossed the 2019 Paris Marathon finish line at the Champs-Élysées. I didn't do it for glory or accolades, and I certainly didn't do it for the nonexistent cheering section waiting for me, or the social media posts that were certain to follow. I did it for me. Because what good is a mantra if you can't or won't live up to it.

During other routine visits to Paris, when I wasn't destroying my body, I began to understand and truly appreciate the rich history of Franco-American relationships. From the American Revolution up through World War II, the histories of our two countries are closely intertwined and sometimes mirrored. A realization that was solidified on a trip to the small town of Romagne-sous-Montfaucon, France.

On Memorial Day, 2019, I was on a road trip through southern France but decided to stop by one of the largest American military cemeteries in Europe, the Meuse-Argonne Military Cemetery, the final resting place of 14,246 military service members—most of whom died during the Meuse-Argonne Offensive of World War I. Pulling into the quaint village, it was chillingly quiet. I would have thought it was abandoned if it weren't for the American flags hanging from every light post and windowsill, a sight that I certainly was not expecting. As I made a right off the main road toward the cemetery, I passed the local church, and as my timing is always impeccable, the church was just getting out. So, I was stuck in my car as hundreds of local villagers left the small yet beautiful stone building. But then instead of heading back to the American flag–adorned homes I had just passed on my way in, the villagers were seemingly walking in the same direction that I was going. I followed them at a snail's pace down the main road and entered the cemetery.

After I parked, I walked up the hill leading to the main amphitheater for what I could see was a ceremony. Reaching the top, I then realized that the entire village had come from the church to a remembrance ceremony to honor the American soldiers buried in the perfectly symmetrical rows on those hallowed grounds. And to add to the chills that I had, lying a foot in front of each headstone were an American and a French flag.

It was a beautiful ceremony, complete with remarks from the local leaders, and an experience that I will never forget. But more importantly, for me, it made me begin to reexamine the way we believe the world views us Americans. I began rereading many of the founding documents of America, from the Constitution to the Treaty of Tripoli, from Alexis De Tocqueville's *Democracy in America* to George Washington's Farewell Address, through a different lens and with a new perspective. And in doing so, coupled with the recent events of the past several years, made a rather profound realization about the state and future of America.

In America, we tend to think that our greatest strengths are our adherence to the rule of law, our democratic institutions, and so on and so forth. But to the rest of the world, and this is something that I had seen before as well, the United States of America isn't just a country or system of government—it's an idea. It's a stalwart beacon of hope for those seeking freedom from oppression. It's a bright light in the darkest of times, and it is the best friend you could ever have, and the worst enemy you would never want.

I came back from Europe in the fall of 2019 with the Washington Nationals about to win their first World Series and a renewed perspective both on my life and on the meaning of America. I've always revered this country for what it was, but for really the first time, I did so for what it could be. So, when I was asked to come be a speaker for a Veterans Day event being hosted by the European Union (EU) delegation to the United States, I absolutely jumped at it.

The day before the event, I had a call with one of the EU staffers who basically told me that I would have three to five minutes to give some remarks. They really made it seem like it would be very casual, informal, and low-key, which was fine by me as I was still a bit jet lagged and getting settled back in DC.

Before the happy hour reception, I attended a symposium hosted by the Atlanta Council featuring the defense minister from Lithuania, Raimundas Karoblis. The panel focused on collective security in Europe, with a specific focus on the Baltic states. Having just seen the problem set of that area, exacerbated by an ever-aggressive Russia and the satellite Russian state of Belarus, I understood many of the tea leaves being dropped by the minister about the current situation in the Baltics—some more pointed than others. But one quote from the defense minister really hit home, and it was that "the hardest and most important currency in international relations is partnerships." It was an anticlimactic quote to the greater "policy wonk" community, but as a practitioner, it was incredibly impactful. As calls for the US to either disband or leave the North Atlantic Treaty Organization (NATO) were increasing in frequency in this period of "America First" isolationism, he was essentially saying doing so was an existential threat to a free Europe.

After visiting the Atlantic Council that morning, I had a couple of hours to kill before I went to the reception on Capitol Hill, so I swung by the Army-Navy Club near Farragut Square to grab a drink and cool off in the air conditioning—DC is after all a swamp. Sitting at the wooden bar, I began to scribble some notes on one of the bar napkins. I hadn't really thought of anything specific to say at the reception other than how much I loved living and traveling in Europe. Maybe I'd tell the story about visiting the Meuse-Argonne Military Cemetery, or one of the various anecdotes I learned about American Revolutionary heroes like the Marquis de Lafayette, Thaddeus Kosciuszko, or Baron von Steuben. But after another cold beer and feeling refreshed, I began writing some high-level bullet points.

My bullets went from the anecdotes of those European immigrants and allies in our fight for independence to more pointed policy statements given the current state of affairs. They went from the talking points I had previously written as an XO at EUCOM, to more fact-based theories I formulated during my travels and experiences across Europe. And after one more beer, you would have thought that I was ready to step onto a stage to give a rebuttal speech at a presidential debate.

Arriving in the Rayburn building later that evening, I made my way to the reception room, where to my surprise, every EU member flag was proudly displayed in front of a rather full crowd. And standing there were nearly every ambassador to the US from those EU members. This was not the informal and "low-key" event I had been told about. After initial pleasantries and the awkward "where do I know you from?" I noticed that the Lithuanian defense minister was there. And next to him was the Lithuanian Ambassador to the United States. And then I recognized several of the Congressional members as they walked in. One I recognized immediately, Representative Joe Wilson (R-SC). I recognized him from President Obama's 2009 State of the Union where he, Joe Wilson, infamously yelled, "You lie!" as the president addressed the joint session of Congress, the American people, and the world. Then the other shoe dropped.

An EU staff member came over to ask if there was anything I needed before my keynote. Wait, what? Apparently the "informal remarks" had somehow morphed into a full keynote address. My response to him was "Nah, I'm all good," but in reality, it was "You're shitting me, right?" The good news is I'm pretty good on my feet. I mean, I was once a political candidate. But being the keynote and last speaker also meant that the bar could be set so high that I might be screwed anyway. And it didn't help that I had a good buzz going from my impromptu happy hour.

Several people spoke, thanked presenting sponsor organizations, and so on. Some others talked about the significance of events like this to recognize not only the importance of international organizations such as NATO and the EU, but also the importance of continuing to forge relationships in the midst of an ever-uncertain global order. And then Joe Wilson got up to the podium. I don't know what I expected, but it certainly wasn't what we got.

Instead of talking about the importance of transatlantic relationships, the EU, NATO, or collective security, Congressman Joe Wilson spent his several minutes talking about the view from his Congressional office—I'm not kidding or embellishing. He joked a bit and floundered about random non sequiturs. If he hadn't been wearing the lapel pin of a member of the United States Congress, I probably would have laughed a bit, but instead I cringed. He then finished his remarks by offering an open invitation for anyone to come by and visit, to check out the view from his office he lamented several times about.

While his remarks were jovial and lighthearted, he certainly didn't heed the warning of "knowing your audience" and provided little to no substance to an audience of ambassadors, diplomats, and other governmental officials who were certainly expecting it.

Adam D. DeMarco

The good news was, I was following him. And the bad news was, I was following him. I looked back down at my half-assed notes and frantically began crossing out lines and scribbling in ideas. I felt like a plebe again, rushing to get my paper finished and turned in on time. But in my frenzy, I had then of course essentially made my half sheet of paper completely illegible.

I don't consider myself a great speaker, and I tend to make every mistake in the presenting book, but the one thing that I am good at is being authentic. So, while I may use my hands, stutter occasionally, or even misuse a word here or there—which I'm quick to correct—my greatest strength is being able to connect with a group, crowd, or audience. And while I don't necessarily get nervous speaking in public, I always keep one main rule in the back of my mind: "don't swear."

After a rather cordial opening of thanking the various organizations and dignitaries in attendance, I took a quick pause and a deep breath, then took the proverbial gloves off. I wasn't about to hold any punches either. The first thing I made perfectly clear was that the greatest existential threats we, the United States, and our international partners face isn't coming from violent extremist organizations like Al-Qaeda, ISIS, Al-Shabab, or Boko Haram. Instead, the greatest threats to self-governing and self-determinant democracies come from the continuous degradation of democratic values and institutions. I spoke about the importance of maintaining the norms of the twenty-first century global order and then culminated with an aptly timed reference to the Lithuanian defense minister I heard earlier that day, who ironically was also now in the room, by referencing his earlier quote that "the hardest and most important currency in international relations is partnerships."

After my rather brief and straightforward remarks, nearly the entire European delegation came over and thanked me for what I said. Were they popular opinions or sentiments from a US standard at that point? Probably not. Keep in mind that President Trump routinely questioned the need for collective security organizations such as NATO. But they were valid, correct, timely, and needed.

Chapter 17

TRUTH & CONSEQUENCES

In May 1802, several months after signing the Military Peace Establishment Act that created the United States Military Academy at West Point, President Thomas Jefferson signed an act that incorporated the District of Columbia and launched the District of Columbia militia to protect the relatively newly founded capital city and the United States government. The impetus behind this was the fear of using military power to influence or impede the legislative process. From this early militia that included Francis Scott Key, the famed writer of "The Star-Spangled Banner," was born the modern-day District of Columbia National Guard (DCNG).

The DCNG has a unique role, responsibility, and authority as it is the only national guard unit that reports to the president of the United States. Initially established to ensure that no other state militia could impede the work and function of the federal government, the DCNG has participated in nearly every major campaign since the founding of the United States. After World War II, and pursuant to Executive Order 10030, the authority to mobilize and deploy the DCNG was then given to the Secretary of Defense (SecDef), who then delegated the command-and-control authorities to the Secretaries of the Army (SecArmy) and Air Force (SecAF) for respective land component and air component matters.

Adam D. DeMarco

The District of Columbia National Guard's mission as it is stands today is to "meet the expectations of the Department of Defense, our Federal and District of Columbia government partners, and the needs of our fellow citizens." Comprised of approximately 2,700 soldiers and airmen, the DCNG aids a litany of partners and missions with what is a relatively small force given the sensitivity, nature, and complexity of the AO in the National Capital Region (NCR). In early 2020, as the world began dealing with the onset of the saga of the global pandemic beset by SARS-CoV-2 (COVID-19), the service members of DCNG would be tested to their very core.

In February 2020, I was activated to support the District of Columbia's COVID-19 response efforts as an operations officer and emergency support planner. My assignment would include working with several local hospitals to ensure that they could manage the logistical and operational challenges if the most dangerous forecasts proved right and there was a surge in COVID-19 patients and ultimately deaths. The reason why we were brought in was to not only assist the medical personnel, but because one of the core competencies and greatest strengths of the entire United States military is our ability to move people and equipment. And with us working side-by-side with medical professionals, we could then assist in moving patients, ventilators, or even decedents.

I was tasked with this mission for several weeks, which then turned to months. During that time, we continued to prepare for what we thought was an inevitable surge of cases. Other members of the DC National Guard along with the Army Corps of Engineers built a state-of-the-art hospital in the Walter E. Washington Convention Center, but thankfully we never had to use it. Then this mission quickly changed on May 29, 2020.

George Floyd was murdered on May 25, 2020. Shortly after, the video of his murder went viral. On May 26, protests began popping up across the city as Americans demanded justice for this blatant act. On the 28th, Governor Tim Walz of Minnesota activated the Minnesota National Guard. And then on the 29th, Derek Chauvin, a former Minneapolis police officer who was fired for his actions days before, was arrested and charged with third-degree murder and second-degree manslaughter for Floyd's death.

On May 29, lockdown restrictions from COVID-19 had just been lifted in DC. So instead of hosting our typical Friday "virtual happy hour," I had some of my friends over for pizza and beer. Before they arrived, I had seen news footage of volatile and aggressive protestors outside of the White House. These violent protestors were hurling objects at members of the United States Secret Service (USSS) and United States Park Police (USPP), and there were reports of protestors throwing caustic substances at officers. As the situation spiraled out of control, both the Secret Service and Park Police were concerned that they would be quickly overrun. Therefore, at some point during that initial chaotic afternoon and into the night, President Trump was ushered into the secure bunker in the White House for safety.

Over the next few days, those protests would increase both in size and volatility. This escalating situation caused the commanding general, Major General William Walker, to order an encampment for the DC National Guard—which means he essentially ordered the soldiers and airmen of the Guard to assume full-time military status because of an in-extremis situation or crisis. I had already been on orders supporting the COVID-19 mission—as were hundreds of others—so this then caused us to put a "tactical pause" on one operation to focus on the other. This was also the first time in my career with the DCNG that we had been "encamped," but unfortunately this wouldn't be the last.

Over the next two days, the DC Guard would rapidly deploy security forces to protect and secure key sites and infrastructure in and across Washington, DC. This included iconic spots like the Lincoln Memorial, the Washington Monument, other key infrastructure sites, and of course, the White House. Meanwhile, open-source news and social media feeds were showing groups of violent protestors looting various areas of DC, including historic Georgetown and the posh area called City Center. Those scenes absolutely bothered me and sent me in a spiral of anger because I also knew that most violent acts weren't perpetrated by protestors demonstrating their First Amendment rights, but rather by anarchists and radicals that wanted nothing more than to create mayhem. But nothing made me angrier than when I received the first reports that service members were injured at Lafayette Square—not to discount the dozens of law enforcement officers from the Park Police and Secret Service who were also hurt during the riots of May 29–31, 2020

On June 1, I was working at my office in nearby Fort Belvoir, Virginia, when I got a notification to return to the DC Armory, located a stone's throw away from my house. Upon arriving, I was nearly immediately tasked to serve as a liaison between the DCNG and USPP for what we all prepared for would be an extremely chaotic afternoon. The previous evening, all hell had broken loose. I was there that night in a different capacity, escorting another officer, essentially being a "battle buddy" for someone as they traversed what felt like a battlefield.

My greatest concern was if a soldier was by themselves, either standing a post or driving a vehicle, that they may have been spotted and attacked by these radical extremists. And I wasn't the only one who felt that way. Acting as this unofficial escort on May

31, and in this ad hoc capacity, I was there when the first flames were lit at St. John's Church, and I was there when the first tear gas canister was fired at Lafayette Square. So, as we mounted the vehicles, I was expecting that we were going into the mouth of the beast for all intents and purposes. If the previous night was any indicator, the torch was already lit, and the tinder marinated in gasoline.

A few hours before I arrived at Lafayette Square on June 1, President Trump along with Secretary of Defense Mark Esper and Attorney General Bill Barr convened a call with governors across the states in what in transcripts published nearly instantaneously seemed like a generic federal update brief if it had been given by General George S. Patton at the Battle of the Bulge.

> "There's no retribution. So, I say that, and the word is dominated. If you don't dominate your city and your state, they're going to walk away with you. And we're doing it in Washington and DC. And we're going to do something that people haven't seen before, but you got to have total domination." – President Donald J. Trump, June 1, 2020

The events over the next twelve to forty-eight hours have been examined, investigated, and reported on across the world by nearly every journalist, watchdog, and governmental agency. They have been the subject of political debate, cantankerous media panels, and even discussed in academic textbooks. And while everyone will have an opinion as to what occurred, when, and why, there are several facts that are undisputable and have been corroborated under oath in sworn testimony, in the press, and in retrospective books by partisan and nonpartisan officials alike.

The first fact is that on Sunday, May 31, the protest at Lafayette Square was by all shapes and shades a violent riot, and those violent actors, criminals, radicals, and extremists were not there in support of or exercising their First Amendment rights or the right to assemble. Instead, they saw this as an opportunity to commit crimes, stoke fear, and attack national landmarks and iconic images of America.

The second fact is that the next day, June 1, while we were all on edge about the potential for the same type of violent riots, the atmosphere was completely different. Unlike the previous night where projectiles including bricks, fireworks, and caustic substances were being hurled at USPP, USSS, other federal agencies, and us, the next day, June 1, was—for the most part—peaceful.

The third fact is that given the peaceful nature of June 1, 2020, the violent clearing of protestors from Lafayette Square was both a surprise to me and a shock to the people exercising their First Amendment rights. Yes, the protestors—who, once again I say, were largely peaceful—were warned to clear the area by the incident commander of the USPP, however by all accounts, both from witnesses and the media, none of the warnings were clear or audible enough to be heard, understood, and reacted to.

And finally, the fourth fact is that riot control agents such as tear gas and other nonlethal munitions were in fact used during the clearing of Lafayette Square. This was initially denied by several federal officials and representatives, but later confirmed both by agencies and by other federal officials—however, once they were no longer in office.

So that afternoon, as President Trump was concluding his public remarks—after his highly contentious call with governors earlier—the order was given to clear Lafayette Square. The cliché is that a photograph says a thousand words, then how many would live television, social feeds, and nearly anyone with a smartphone say? Well, here's my account, sworn under oath, of what happened next.

> "A few minutes before 6:00 pm, I was standing near the statue of Andrew Jackson in the middle of Lafayette Square as DC National Guard personnel formed up behind Park Police units positioned in a line behind the perimeter fence on the H Street side of the square, facing demonstrators on the other side of the fence. From what I could observe, the demonstrators were behaving peacefully, exercising their First Amendment rights.
>
> At approximately 6:05 pm, after I had repositioned myself close to the line, I observed Attorney General William Barr and Chairman of the Joint Chiefs of Staff, General Mark Milley, walking across Lafayette Square from the direction of the White House toward the security perimeter on H Street. Attorney General Barr walked right up to the line of Park Police and DC National Guard, in front of the demonstrators, then walked down the line of Park Police officers and National Guardsmen.
>
> The Attorney General then headed toward the statue of President Jackson where he appeared to confer with Park Police officers. General Milley walked toward the area where I was standing. As the senior National Guard officer on the scene at the time, I gave General Milley a quick briefing on our mission and the current situation. General Milley asked for an estimate of the number of demonstrators, and I estimated 2,000. General Milley told me to ensure that National Guard personnel remained calm, adding that we were there to respect the

demonstrators' First Amendment rights.

At around 6:20 pm, after the Attorney General and General Milley departed Lafayette Square, the Park Police issued the first of three warning announcements to the demonstrators, directing them to disperse. I did not expect the announcements so early, as the curfew was not due to go into effect until 7:00 pm, 40 minutes later. The warnings were conveyed using a megaphone near the statue of President Jackson, approximately 50 yards from the demonstrators. From where I was standing, approximately 20 yards from the demonstrators, the announcements were barely audible, and I saw no indication that the demonstrators were cognizant of the warnings to disperse.

At approximately 6:30 pm, the Park Police began the clearing operation, led by Civil Disturbance Units and horse-mounted officers. The Secret Service, and other law enforcement agencies I was unable to identify, also participated in the push. No National Guard personnel participated in the push or engaged in any other use of force against the demonstrators. By then I had moved to the northeast corner of Lafayette Square near the statue of General Kosciuszko. As the clearing operation began, I heard explosions and saw smoke being used to disperse the protestors.

The Park Police liaison officer told me that the explosions were "stage smoke," and that no tear gas was being deployed against the demonstrators. But I could feel irritation in my eyes and nose, and based on my previous exposure to tear gas in my training at West Point and later in my Army training, I recognized that irritation as effects consistent with CS or "tear gas." And later that evening, I found spent tear gas cannisters on the street nearby.

During the initial push, I had relocated to a position near the northeast corner of Lafayette Square, next to the Comfort Station that had been burned the previous evening, in order to closely observe the clearing operation. As the horses began to move from east to west along H Street, they stopped in the vicinity of St. John's Church and the Park Police's Civil Disturbance Unit then took the lead and pushed the demonstrators further down H Street. From my vantage point, I saw demonstrators scattering and fleeing as the Civil Disturbance Unit charged toward them. I observed people fall to the ground as some Civil Disturbance Unit members used their shields offensively as weapons. As I walked behind the Civil Disturbance Units pushing westward on H Street, I also observed unidentified law enforcement personnel behind our National Guardsmen using "paintball-like" weapons to discharge what I later learned to be "pepper balls" into the crowd, as demonstrators continued to retreat.

About ten minutes after the clearing operation began, the Park Police ordered the DC National Guard to move up behind the Park Police clearing elements pushing north on Vermont Avenue, 16th Street, and Connecticut Avenue to reinforce and relieve the Park Police on the newly established northern perimeter. I took up a position on 16th Street between St. John's Church and the AFL-CIO building.

By then, H Street had been cleared of demonstrators. Soon thereafter, several black sport utility vehicles pulled up at the intersection of 16th Street and H Street, and uniformed Secret Service 5 officers began to establish an inner security cordon between the SUVs and our perimeter on I Street. At around 7:05 pm, I saw the President walking onto H Street from Lafayette Square, near St. John's Church, accompanied by his security detail." *–Testimony to the United States Congress*, July 28, 2020

Nearly every field grade army officer has studied Carl von Clausewitz, who is often regarded as the foremost mind on military strategy, and has spent hours combing through his defining work *On War*. In it, Clausewitz talks about the "fog of war" and defines this as "the realm of uncertainty; three quarters of the factors on which action in war is based are wrapped in a fog of greater or lesser uncertainty." In essence, for a military officer, this means that you will never see the full picture during an operation, and it's only after that we can gain clarity about the actions on the objective. And later that night, that fog lifted, and I was sickened, embarrassed, and angry at what I saw.

Chapter 18

THE HARDER RIGHT

I got back to the armory much later that evening, exhausted. The pungent odor of tear gas lingered on my sweat-soaked uniform—it was after all summer in the swamp. But I was not only physically tired, but emotionally drained. After the clearing occurred, and the DCNG established the perimeter—essentially holding the security line for hours—what you may not know of is that our soldiers—of all genders and races—were on the receiving end of hours of verbal abuse by our fellow Americans.

There was one specific instance where one of our soldiers, a young black kid, was being berated by a group of black kids, being called such things as "Uncle Tom"—a historically derogatory epithet dating back to 1852—and much, much worse. These agitators were right up in his face. Close enough that every time they swore at him the spit from their hateful words landed on his face shield.

I saw what was occurring and began to walk over, as did other NCOs who were nearby. To this soldier's credit, he stood there, poised, collected, proud of who he was and what he represented. Me, well, I probably would have lost my cool at the first slurred syllable from those kids and made front-page news. This soldier probably could have withstood this verbal assault all night, but no one should be on the receiving end of something like that—

especially from someone who may have been your neighbor, classmate, colleague, or friend. I went to one of the nearby NCOs and told them to pull him off the security line and replace him. Another soldier came over and tapped him on the shoulder to signal he was being replaced. I then watched as the young soldier walked back behind our lines, took a seat on a nearby bench, took his helmet off and began to break down and cry. My heart broke for him. There were no words I could say that would take that pain away. So, I walked over and simply patted him on the back of the head and handed him a bottle of water, saying, "Well done."

With those images fresh in my mind, as I walked into the armory to drop off my radio and take off my gear, I turned my phone on for the first time in a while. Nearly instantaneously, as I was walking through the door where I was dropping my equipment off, it was bombarded with notifications. I quickly glanced at them, my vision a bit blurry from fatigue, but almost every sentence contained two words: "Trump" and "Bible."

Between the time when Lafayette Square was cleared and when I first saw the president walking toward St. John's Church, I assumed that something had happened. I don't know exactly what I assumed, but something must have occurred. Maybe there was a gunshot? Maybe there was an imminent threat such as an IED or S-VEST? I just assumed that there was something that occurred that triggered this. Would that explain why the president was walking by the church, followed closely behind by nearly his entire cabinet? Who knows? Well, as I began to read some of the still-being-updated articles from the *New York Times*, *Washington Post*, and others, I began to realize the gravity of the situation, and the full weight of what occurred felt like a ton of bricks had just been thrust on my shoulders.

The next day, June 2, Admiral Mike Mullen, former Chairman

of the Joint Chiefs, wrote a scathing article in *The Atlantic* titled "I Cannot Remain Silent." The photo on the article was of our soldiers, moving north up 16th Street to relieve the law enforcement officers who cleared the street, followed by his first sentence, which felt like a dagger thrust into my heart: "It sickened me yesterday to see security personnel—including members of the National Guard—forcibly and violently clear a path through Lafayette Square to accommodate the president's visit outside St. John's Church."

Wait, what? That's not at all what happened. In a day and age where perception is reality based off tweets, likes, and comments, where a vitriolic meme can travel twice around the world before a person can even offer a defense, the former Chairman of the Joint Chiefs essentially called out, confirmed, and then eviscerated the very soldiers he used to lead. Clausewitz's fog had barely settled, and he already had served as a one-man judge and jury as to what happened and who was guilty. Moreover, I was extremely disturbed to think that this narrative was now out there for others to latch onto. That my own friends and family, fellow service members and colleagues, may think that we did that. And I was heartbroken for my fellow soldiers, like the kid who we pulled off the line, who served honorably and did their job, that they were now being plunged into this global scandal that was unfolding before our very eyes.

But if that wasn't enough, then I saw the statement from Acting United States Park Police Chief Gregory T. Monahan, of which a specific line caught my attention: "USPP officers and other assisting law enforcement partners did not use tear gas or OC Skat Shells to close the area at Lafayette Park."

I thought to myself, "What in the actual $@*% is happening!?"

In those following days, I felt absolutely gutted about

everything. And if what actually occurred—the violent force against peaceful protestors—wasn't enough, the incessant lying from nearly every organization and agency that was there, about virtually everything, simply put me over the edge. My emotions turned to anger, anger at our leadership, my leadership, hell, anger at anyone who could have and should have made a stand about what was right. Yes, human beings are complicated people, we are messy. There are lots of gray areas in life, a lot of external factors, and even more second- and third-order consequences. However, for as much gray area as there is, there are also universal truths. The universal truth, or natural law, between good and evil, between right and wrong, and between the truth and lies. In the military, we don't live, work, or operate in a world of "alternative facts." Instead, we are and must be held accountable for our actions— everything we do and fail to do—because that's what leadership truly is. Which is why I couldn't for the life of me fathom what was occurring before all our eyes.

There's no way I was the only person feeling like this, was I? If there's one thing I learned from my previous battles with mental health, it is that people tend to suffer in silence. I began, quietly, reaching out to some of the soldiers who were out there on that mission just to gauge how they were and see how they were doing. In full transparency, it was half to ensure they were all right and half to see if my feelings were justified and shared. To my surprise, the nearly resounding uniform response to my inquiries was, "Sir, roger, I'm good. And, yes, FUBAR."

There's a stark difference between being in combat, dealing with life-or-death threats from an enemy, and being in the middle of Washington, DC, in the "Capital of the Free World," watching peaceful civilians, Americans, get violently attacked by their own government. Seeing all this, from people using riot shields as weapons to indiscriminately shooting civilians with pepper ball guns, happen to Americans—our neighbors, families, and friends—has a different effect on a person from being in combat against an enemy of the United States. For instance, looting and burning a church has a much greater emotional impact than doing the same at a convenience store—an analogy I would find myself using again in a completely different, yet similar, situation.

On June 11, General Mark Milley held a virtual address to the graduating officers from the National Defense University; it was still COVID-19 times. Along with providing some inspiring and insightful remarks, he took the time to address the elephant in the room. He bluntly and unequivocally stated that he should not have been at Lafayette Square. And with a sense of humility yet sternness, he explained that his presence created an image of military involvement in domestic politics. And while he touted the work of the National Guard across the United States, he finished with a quote that stuck with me: "Embrace the Constitution… Keep it close to your heart. It is our North Star; it is our map to a better future."

At West Point, we live under the Cadet Honor Code, which states that "a Cadet will not lie, cheat, or steal, or tolerate those who do." Ironically, my "firstie" (senior) year, I lived above the Honor Monument in Eisenhower Barracks. But anyone who has ever had to live by and inculcate the Cadet Honor Code can attest that the hardest part of the code is not refraining from lying, cheating, or stealing. Rather, it's tolerating. Because at West Point, we are engrained in the fundamental idea that if you turn a blind eye to an honor violation, and you do nothing about it, you're just as guilty as the person committing it. The West Point Cadet Prayer addresses this conflict of conscience: "Make us to choose the harder right instead of the easier wrong, and never to be content with a half-truth when the whole can be won."

There wasn't a definitive time or event that made me say, "That's it. I'm going to become a whistleblower." And being a "whistleblower" was certainly not on my 2020 vision board, nor was it a lifelong goal of mine. But after several conversations, some intense meetings, and through absolutely wild circumstances, I was advised to seek whistleblower status under the Military Whistleblower Protection Act to provide context, background, and direct knowledge as to the events of June 1, 2020, and to, what I viewed as, a gross and unnecessary escalation and use of force against peaceful American citizens exercising their First Amendment rights.

Under this status and with legal representation, I provided protected communications to the United States Congress as they conducted their constitutional duty of providing oversight of the executive branch specific to the actions at Lafayette Square. Many of these communications were simply used for background to understand the scope and ensure lawmakers and the American public writ large knew that we, the National Guard, did nothing improper, immoral, or illegal at Lafayette Square.

Article I of the Constitution outlines the roles and responsibilities of the United States Congress, and their duty to conduct oversight of federal agencies. This responsibility inherently gets politicized all too often, and the functional power of that oversight responsibility becomes relegated to taking arguments to the media instead of to the chambers. That said, during the Trump administration, there were what seemed like a record number of "anonymous sources" reaching out to the press to shine a light on issues, actions, or scandals. I didn't want any part of that. If I was to do anything, I wanted it to be strictly by the book, to not only protect myself from any negative attacks or impropriety, but to also ensure that our soldiers, units, and organizations would not bear the brunt of these same attacks. So, for one of the very few times in my life, I colored within the lines and stayed within the parameters of what I understood as the Whistleblower Protection Act and, more importantly, what my new counsel, Mr. David Laufman, advised.

After several back-and-forth electronic communications, I was asked to sit for a virtual conference with members of the House Committee of Natural Resources. This committee was conducting an after-action review of what occurred not only because it occurred at a National Historic Landmark, but also because the USPP falls under the oversight of this committee. I hesitantly agreed, and after hours of what felt like a deposition—it was under oath as all communications to the US Congress are—I felt like I had said my piece. But then the next request came: would I be willing to say my piece, again, in front of the committee, live, televised, and essentially, for the world to hear directly?

My answer was quick. It wasn't just a no, but it was a "$@*% no." Sure, I'll provide the committee information in their constitutional duties, but not at the expense of me, my life, and my career. Meaning, as I provided protected communications, my identity was duty-bound to be protected. But the second I step out of that protected shadow, by either writing an opinion editorial (OP-ED) or, in this case, by testifying in public, it then becomes open season on me, my life, and my future.

And to further solidify my position, I had absolutely nothing to gain if I were to testify in public. You'd think that a kid who was in numerous school talent shows and musicals and who, in his prime, was the high school homecoming king would relish this opportunity. Some people think that any press is good press, well, not me. Partly because I don't want to let my parents down, but also because the thick skin I think I have is quite thin and brittle these days due to my previous endeavors, which leads to my main opposition to going public. I was a political candidate for public office only two years earlier! There is no universe where me coming forward would be a good idea.

There was absolutely no upside to this for me. Because on the one hand, I'm just a political operative, using this situation to conduct a political attack against the administration. And on the other, and the other side of the aisle, I'm just an opportunistic hack, a one-time-failed candidate seeking another trip around the sun. But then there was the reality of the situation. I was the only person who was coming forward. I was probably the only person who could talk to the events, the actions, and what did or did not happen. And moreover, I was one of the only people bound by an oath to the Constitution, "to support and defend the Constitution of the United States," and only the Constitution. So, I had a decision to make.

What I've realized is that there's never a convenient time to do the right thing. And sometimes even doing the right thing comes at a cost. And in this case, I knew it would be both personally and professionally. I also knew that in the end, when the dust settled from all of this, that I would be the one who would have to look at myself in the mirror. Was I willing to throw everything away, my professional career, personal life, ambitions, dreams, and future for what I believed was morally right?

I spent the next few days in a sleepless stupor. My heart continuously racing. I had a decision to make, and no matter what I did or who I prayed to, I hadn't received any clarity on what to do. So, I did what any nerdy, idealistic insomniac would do: I began to binge-watch my all-time favorite show, Aaron Sorkin's *The West Wing*.

In the final episode of season two, called "Two Cathedrals," President Josiah Bartlet, played by Martin Sheen, is dealing with several crises: a situation overseas, the death of his dear friend and secretary, a scandal involving his own health, and ultimately the decision of whether he will seek another term. As Bartlet and his staff wrangle and deal with these various issues, throughout the episode Sorkin cuts back to previous memories of Bartlet's life, specifically highlighting his now deceased former secretary Mrs. Dolores Landingham's impact on his life.

As the episode draws to a close after the funeral of Mrs. Landingham, Bartlet is seen in the Oval Office at the White House, as a storm rips about outside. The wind gusts and startingly opens one of the doors, at which point Bartlet yells out for Mrs. Landingham. She then appears as a vision to Bartlet, who has already made his decision not to run for reelection, and peppers him with questions about the state of the union and the country. And finally, as Bartlet rattles off statistic after statistic, she says to the president:

> "You know, if you don't want to run again, I respect that. But if you don't run 'cause you think it's gonna be too hard or you think you're gonna lose—well, God, Jed, I don't even want to know you." – *The West Wing*, Episode 2, Season 2

I've spent my life waiting for opportunities and looking for signs. Sometimes I follow them, sometimes I don't. Sometimes I'm right, many times I'm wrong. But I have never failed to meet a challenge, have never backed down when my back is against the wall, and have never quit. The next day, I texted David Laufman and simply said, "Let's do it."

Chapter 19

THE SPOTLIGHT

The week leading up to the hearing was terrifying. While there had been more highly publicized hearings in recent months featuring Lieutenant Colonel Alexander Vindman, this hearing was different. Because not only was it a committee that had some interesting characters, a la Representatives Louie Gohmert (R-TX) and Paul Gosar (R-AZ), but I also had to walk the tightrope of public opinion. This wasn't a safe space, and in my mind, I was preparing to be cannon fodder for both sides.

My lawyer and several of his colleagues peppered me with rigorous "murder board" sessions. Testing my recollection of events, questioning my knowledge of rules and regulations, and trying to rattle me with personal attacks. It was a train up for a bout that I thought was going to be the main card of the day.

When I was "noticed," meaning that it was made public that I was going to testify, an interesting thing happened. Around the same time, it was announced that Attorney General Bill Barr would testify on the same day to the House Judiciary Committee. It would be Barr's first public testimony to a committee that had been trying to question him for over a year. I don't believe in coincidences either. And it just so happens that on the same day that I would provide information related to Lafayette Square, the Attorney General would be in the hot seat as well. I immediately went from the main event to the undercard.

The morning of July 28, 2020, was like any other morning in the COVID-19 era. Except in a mere few hours, I'd be front and center of a congressional firing squad. I went down to the gym and got a quick workout in, trying at all costs to avoid any morning cable news channels. I didn't want or need any distractions. My dad had flown up—like he always has—to be my support for this. After a morning workout that did nothing to lessen my stress, of course I walk back into my apartment to see my dad sitting in front of the television watching MSNBC's *Morning Joe*. Typical.

As I steamed my shirt and tie for the hundredth time, I rehearsed my opening remarks. I could have gone on for days with flowery poetry about the values of military officers, and the sanctity of our oath of office, then hit the punch lines of rules of engagement (ROE) and rules for the use of force (RUF), but given that I only had five minutes, I had to "be brief, be bold, be gone." After numerous revisions between myself and David, we arrived at a happy medium for my prepared remarks, sticking with the themes of "here's a timeline, here's what I saw, thanks for your time."

Arriving to the Longworth building that day was strange and walking in to testify was like a movie. As I entered the committee room, Acting Park Police Chief Gregory Monahan was there in his uniform with his team of lawyers. I could sense in many ways that they looked at me as the enemy. Words didn't have to convey it; their scowls in my direction were more than enough.

One interesting decision that my lawyer and I made was that I would not testify in uniform. As I was not under subpoena and essentially had responded to a voluntary request, I did not want to drag the military into this mess. And taking from General Milley's comments from June 11, where he stated that the military should always be seen and remain apolitical, and fully knowing that a line of questioning would focus in part on my previous candidacy for office, I wanted to have a large firewall between attacking a guy in a suit and attacking a military officer in uniform.

Over a week earlier, longtime civil rights activist and titan of the United States Congress John Lewis passed away, and on the same day that I was testifying, he would be lying in state in the Capitol Rotunda. I never met the legendary man but knew of the heroism he continuously displayed throughout his life in the face of adversity, overwhelming odds, and danger. He was famous for the phrase "good trouble," but there was one line that he said that was forged in my mind.

> "When you see something that is not right, not just, not fair, you have a moral obligation to say something. To do something." – Representative John Lewis

At the eleventh hour, I decided to include this quote in the end of my statement, both to honor his legacy and to drive home the point of me being before the committee. Not for the committee, but for those who might hear my voice, read my words, or one day learn about this event in history books.

After I concluded my opening remarks, sitting before the committee, the bell rang, and as they say, "we got it on." First up was Representative Louie Gohmert. He was a former Army lawyer turned Texas judge and later, a congressman. What the members of the committee probably didn't know was that I had done some "opposition research" on all of them to try to get some insight into what they might ask, how they might ask it, and what pitfalls they might try to get me to fall into. I also learned of some digs on them and, in my juvenile dreams, concocted some witty responses, which would have landed flat in the committee room but would have made me laugh later. Knowing that Rep. Gohmert was a former Army lawyer in the Judge Advocate General Corps, I knew that he would first hit me on being a Democrat then try berating me as an Army officer.

The key to congressional hearings is that they are never in favor of the witness. The members have all the advantages and the leverage. There's no winning in appearing before a committee; the best outcome is that you can come out with your head held high and the ability to look yourself in the mirror afterward. So as Rep. Gohmert tried to entice me into a back-and-forth over my registration as a Democrat or how I was indicative of a cultural shift within the military, or just asserting that he was a better-tougher-smarter-stronger person than I, I just provided as short and concise responses as possible, followed by the word "sir." His frustration in not being able to get me to tango with him in the committee room and the online court of public opinion was evident, as he then shifted focus and went on a tirade about General Milley and his statements from June 11. As he finished his line of questioning, yielding his time and signaling that I survived the first round, in my head, I visualized myself chiming in with a snarky "Thank you for your service." If only I could go back in time.

But then the hearing got interesting. While the Republicans despised me as a political operative, some of the Democrats saw me in many ways as an opportunist. Whereas the Acting Park Police Chief was questioned for nearly two hours, my questioning was finished in nearly thirty minutes. Many of the topics that I had prepared to speak about, such as RUF, crowd control tactics, and so on, were barely mentioned. I had prepared, thanks to David, for a litany of questions that would focus on codified doctrine for civil disturbances and had a binder full of Army Doctrine

Publications (ADP) containing manuals from civil disturbance procedures to the use of riot control agents. I had pages earmarked, standards highlighted, and was ready at the first inclination to provide doctrinal answers to what I hoped would be not only an opportunity to clear our soldiers of any wrongdoing, but also to call out the egregiousness of what occurred that day.

But instead, the focus of my short-lived questioning was on helicopters, my background, or things that had nothing to do with the topic or incident at hand—par for the course of the United States Congress. At one point, the chairman of the committee even included a photo from my Instagram account of me in the locker room at the 2008 Army-Navy Game with President George W. Bush. Was this it? Was this what I risked my personal and professional reputation for? And sadly, it was.

During his earlier testimony, the Acting Park Police Chief put a brick and a helmet on the table, to serve as a representation of the violence that occurred. There was only one issue: that violence occurred on the preceding days and not on June 1. The argument that the chief was seemingly making was that because of the violence of Saturday and Sunday, the situation dictated that the Park Police act with force. Essentially saying that because the two previous nights were riots, they, the Park Police, had to preempt that violence with violence. That's not security, that's vengeance and dare I say retribution.

Leaving the hearing, rather dismayed at the lack of constructive questioning, and left with a feeling of "that was it?!" David, my dad, and I went to pay our respects to the late John Lewis at the Capitol. Shortly after, having thanked David for all his guidance, wisdom, counsel, and friendship, my dad and I caught a ride to my apartment to change and then grab an anticlimactic celebratory lunch at the Old Ebbitt Grill. Although all eyes were on the attorney general, whose hearing started around the same time that I began testifying, my phone had already been blowing up with calls, text messages, and direct messages from news producers trying to get me on one of their cable news shows that night. Balancing this tightrope situation of walking the straight and narrow, not wanting to be the opportunist everyone already thought I was, and not jeopardizing my protected whistleblower status, David, my dad, and I collectively made the decision that I would not do any press. I came out, said my piece, provided fact-based testimony, and now would slowly fade away. The only thing I wanted out of any of this—the testifying in public piece—was nothing.

Instead, I politely had to decline the opportunity to speak with some of my favorite journalists by giving them the old "sorry, but I have dinner plans with my dad." The producer on the receiving end probably thought I was an idiot for saying that, but for my dad and me, as we rode in an uber through DC, we had a good laugh. Walking back into my apartment, I greeted my dog, George, who did not realize the gravity of what just occurred. I threw my backpack on the counter and rinsed out my coffee mug as my dad turned on the television only to see Attorney General Bill Barr filling the screen. And as my heart rate had finally, after days and weeks, gotten to a resting rate, it suddenly spiked again when I heard the name "Major DeMarco."

Representative Pramila Jayapal (D-WA) asked the attorney general of the United States, the top law enforcement official in the country, to respond to the fact that I had just testified about the excessive use of force at Lafayette Square. And the attorney general, without skipping a beat, said, "I don't remember Captain DeMarco, who is the same Captain DeMarco who ran as a Democratic candidate for Congress in Maryland..."

While some people might have taken that slight and demotion

from major to captain as a personal affront, I found it quite comical and insightful. For one, it went to show that the attorney general, the top law enforcement official in the United States, had his team of advisors not only investigate my background but then prepare him to respond to something said or asked about me, the major, the whistleblower from Lafayette Square. And then the second piece was that he was so concerned with what I might say that he was already positioned to personally attack me and label me as a partisan actor. It was both a comical yet terrifying five minutes, my dad siding on the former and me certainly the latter.

There's a famous quote that is mistakenly attributed to Winston Churchill: "You have enemies? Good. That means you've stood up for something, sometime in your life." Unfortunately, this quote has been debunked by the International Churchill Society as one the former prime minister never gave. But, if he had, it would probably serve as the mantra for the rest of my life, or certainly at least my next tattoo. Quickly after the hearing, and in the following weeks and months, where I simply just tried to do the right thing, I had earned my fair share of enemies. I felt like I was adorned with another scarlet letter, a "W" for whistleblower.

In the following months, several reports were issued that tried to shed light on what occurred June 1, but they only seemed to seek to exonerate culpability for the actions of that day. The Department of Homeland Security refused to conduct an internal investigation as to the actions of its department, which included members of the Bureau of Prisons, Customs and Border Patrol, and others involved in the events of June 1. The Department of Interior, which has jurisdiction over the United States Park Police, conducted an internal investigation with which I cooperated. To their credit, they were able to determine that I had made a wrong observation in my testimony, to which I concede they are correct, given the evidence.

The first was that the Park Police Incident Commander did in fact use a Long-Range Acoustic Device (LRAD) in giving audible warnings. My testimony was that, given my location, my line of sight, and the audibility and sound of the announcements, I believed they came from a megaphone. Given the report from the Department of Interior and their evidence, the announcements were given using an LRAD. However, the report also notes that the Park Police were not familiar with the piece of equipment, and therefore it was used only on loudspeaker mode—meaning it acted only as a megaphone—which is why it was barely audible. Another observation was that the non-scalable fence that I said arrived later the evening of June 1, 2020, was in fact already there in the vicinity of Lafayette Square. However, it was out of my eyesight, therefore I never saw it, so I never knew it.

I will also concede that while I call the area where the events of June 1, 2020, occurred Lafayette Square, the National Park Service refers to it as Lafayette Park. From my research, the difference is the park is the actual park in the middle of the square, as the square also includes the adjacent roads and buildings. Thankfully, that was not a line of questioning during my quizzical testimony.

But the million-dollar question is, did or did not the president of the United States order the violent clearing of Lafayette Square?

Based on the facts that I know, no.

Based on the opinion I have made from those facts, no.

I believe that the events and actions of June 1, 2020, resulted from a massive calamity of errors across the board and across every federal agency that was there that day.

The perimeter should have been established earlier on in the day, and I believe the plan was to do so. The reason it wasn't was because of a lack of personnel to establish a new security perimeter, and it wasn't until we, the DCNG, showed up later in the early evening that they, the USPP, then had the necessary amount of personnel to clear the area. But given the time frame, and that the president already had plans for his photo, the USPP leadership on the ground made the decision to clear the area in a rapid and violent nature to expedite the process and ensure that the president's "photo op" would not be impeded. The USPP had to, as Secretary Mark Esper said, "dominate the battle space."

Unfortunately, the most important part about all of this gets lost in the finger pointing and the "he-said-she-said" semantics of domestic politics. And that is that on June 1, Americans were largely peacefully exercising their First Amendment rights and were subjected to a violent attack from law enforcement in the shadow of the White House. In the capital of the United States, and in the capital of the free world, a free people's government forcefully and violently removed them to facilitate the movement of the president.

In the following days, the emails and messages spanned the spectrum from supportive praise to outright death threats; it was, after all, par for the course of this country. My social media information, emails, even official government email addresses were posted, and my entire personal life was virtually doxed. While I was prepared for it on some level and knew that all of this would occur on some scale, it still hurt. The internet and social media, while they aren't real places, can do real damage. But as for me and this controversy, I was ready to ride off into the sunset like the ending of the 1953 Western, *Shane*. And wondering the same questions, how did it or does it really end. These days, I take more solace in the second part of the same John Lewis quote I used in my opening statement to the United States Congress:

> "Our children and their children will ask us, 'What did you do? What did you say?' …we have a mission and a mandate to be on the right side of history." – Rep. John Lewis

Chapter 20

THE INSURRECTION

There isn't a word in the dictionary that describes this feeling. As I stood in the Capitol Rotunda, underneath the watchful eye of the Constantino Brumidi's painting of President George Washington rising to the heavens flanked by the goddesses of Liberty and Victory, *The Apotheosis of Washington*, it was a perfect combination of anger, despair, depression, and yet, hope. Surreal to say the least.

Only twelve hours earlier, a mob had breached the marble walls and, for the first time since 1814, essentially sacked the "Citadel of Democracy," the "People's House," the United States Capitol. And as I stood there, in the hallowed chamber where some of the most important figures in American history had lain in state, I started to put the pieces together of exactly what happened, how it happened, what happens next, and where do we go from here.

On January 1, 2021, after ringing in the New Year by watching Anderson Cooper and Andy Cohen talk about dropping acid on national television, I ordered a pizza and sat in my DC apartment overlooking the Washington Monument. Nothing of significance. I was so absolutely spent with anything that remotely looked like current events, news, world affairs, or politics. 2020, which was thankfully finally over, had been a rollercoaster. From COVID-19 to Lafayette Square, coupled with the personal and professional backlash I faced, I was eager for a fresh start to a new year: "new year, new me, please!"

I had once found randomly scrolling through Instagram feeds and Facebook to be a place of solace and reprieve, but heading into the new year, I tried to make a resolution to do away with the vice that social media had become. From the time frame of June 1, 2020, to January 1, 2021, social media had become even more toxic—if that was even possible—and given that my name had already been sullied, it was probably best for my mental state to not engage in it. I made it only a couple of days into my self-imposed exile before I caught wind of the upcoming "Make America Great Again (MAGA) March" planned for January 6. I thought to myself, "Great, another one…"

Back in November 2020, there had been a "Million MAGA March," about a week after former Vice President Joe Biden was declared President-Elect Joe Biden. I remember because the morning of November 14, the day of the planned march, I was driving to the gym for my Saturday morning workout, and as I drove up 14th Street, through the heart of the District, and while the occasional "Trump 2020" flag didn't stand out, I distinctly remember driving around Logan Circle and for the first time seeing the black and gold flags associated with the heavily armored or "kitted" members of the "Proud Boys."

I was dumbfounded but also almost starstruck. It was the first time I had seen these idiots in the flesh. Coupled together in a small group, they were drinking coffee outside of the Wawa coffee shop. Most of the guys I saw were exactly the type of people I pictured to be part of this far-right, conspiratorial, neo-fascist group. Middle-aged, overweight white guys, the kind who meet you and immediately tell you about their high school football days and claim that they "thought about joining the military, but

. . ." It's a common stereotype and refrain. I drove around Logan Circle twice just to get a good look at these guys, and the second time I thought about yelling a snarky remark. But it's a dangerous thing to trigger a Proud Boy before his morning coffee, so I hear.

That afternoon, during the planned march and demonstration, President Trump, who was declared the loser of the 2020 election a week earlier, took his motorcade by the Million MAGA marchers, providing much-needed encouragement and validation to these groups. That day of protests and demonstrations ended when the Proud Boys, hyped up on the no longer tacit support of the commander in chief, found themselves embroiled in several clashes across the city with counter-protestors. Fights broke out at the Black Lives Matter Plaza, which then spilled into other streets in other areas and ended in dozens of arrests.

Then in early December, the Proud Boys showed up again in DC and wreaked havoc near what had become their de facto headquarters, Harry's Bar, located on the first floor of Hotel Harrington. Unfortunately, Harry's Bar became ground zero for the Proud Boys not because of any other reason than that it was relatively close to the Trump Hotel but had cheaper drinks. Proximity to anything Trump was a drug for this cultish fascist group who fed off the fervor of the commander in chief. For instance, in a September 2020 debate when asked by then Fox News host Chris Wallace to denounce the Proud Boys—who are admittedly a right-wing extremist group—instead of denouncing white supremacist groups once, he infamously said, "Stand back and stand by." However, the owners and workers of both Harry's Bar and Hotel Harrington both explicitly stated that they do not support nor want the support of right-wing extremists.

It was also during this December gathering that Proud Boys members stole the banner that read "#BLACKLIVESMATTER" from the nearby Asbury United Methodist Church, the oldest black Methodist church in the district, and set it ablaze. Enrique Tarrio, a Miami-based extremist apparel peddler and the leader of the Proud Boys, posted a picture of the banner burning to social media, and then brazenly admitted in an interview with the *Washington Post* that he was part of the racially motivated act.

Living only a few blocks from where this all took place, for me, this was all much more of a nuisance than anything else. The Proud Boys and the host of other similarly aligned groups would spend their days driving around DC, honking, waving flags—both the United States and that of the Confederate States—yelling slogans like "Don't Tread on Me" and other random acts of fake patriotism. But to their credit, their numbers and presence were continuously growing.

So, when I became aware that there was going to be another MAGA march on January 6, I expected much of the same extremist violence, but given that their numbers had been increasing and the fact that President Trump himself tweeted about the planned rally on January 6, this seemed a bit different. It was my full expectation, given that the DCNG had been mobilized and encamped numerous times over the summer after June 1, 2020, that we would be under the same activation and mobilization orders.

After Lafayette Square, there was an understandable concern about the optics of the military being involved in civil matters—whether reacting to civil disturbances or simply providing support to civil authorities. Leaders from the DC National Guard up to the Pentagon were rightfully concerned. Because whether it was the DC National Guard or the 82nd Airborne Division, the images of uniform-clad soldiers with "U.S. ARMY" name tapes can create dangerous perceptions. And in today's media world, perception is some people's reality.

After the racially motivated flag burning incident in December, an arrest warrant was placed for Proud Boys' leader Enrique Tarrio. So, when he arrived back in Washington, DC, presumably for the January 6 rally, it should have been no surprise that he was immediately met by local and federal authorities and placed under arrest for vandalism. Unfortunately for him, he was also carrying two high-capacity ammunition magazines, a felony in the district. It was then reported that, while detained, Tarrio stated that the magazines were for someone else, or that he was delivering them to someone who had purchased them. I remember this, because I made a joke to a friend, "Why was the Proud Boys guy carrying mags? Doesn't he just carry White Claws?" "Mags" being the shorthand for magazines, and White Claws being the low-carb seltzers that Tarrio had been photographed carrying in the magazine pouches of his coyote brown tactical vest.

On January 5, the request for assistance from the DC Metro Police Department (DC MPD) was approved, and the mission assignment for the DC National Guard was received, which was then prepared, planned, and distributed to the supporting DCNG units. The overall mission was to support DC MPD by providing traffic control points (TCPs) assistance and establishing blocking positions in certain sectors around the planned demonstration. The DC MPD was, to the best of my knowledge, the only organization to submit a request for assistance and certainly was the only organization that the DCNG would be supporting.

There's lots of speculation about what happened in the days leading up to and on January 6, specifically with the planning or failures to plan, and frankly, I wasn't a part of any of it. As a result of the fallout of my stepping forward about the events of June 1, my testimony, and the questions that resulted from it, I was effectively marginalized, castigated, and silenced. As one officer put it, "[I] am in the penalty box for a while." I wasn't surprised, I knew that was going to happen, and was prepared to be ostracized. However, one thing that did bother me was that many of the leaders who I looked up to, people who I confided in, and many times confided in me, turned their backs on me. Never once asking me about the situation, and from what I can gather, certainly never reading my testimony or hearing my remarks. But nevertheless, to make light of my situation, and thanks to Attorney General Bill Barr, at least I could say, "Well, I've been disliked and hated by much more important people."

On January 6, knowing that the roads were going to be shut down between 14th Street and Constitution Avenue, I opted to work out in my apartment building. If my entire life sounds like it revolves around the gym, you wouldn't be right, but you wouldn't be completely wrong either. After my workout, I decided to venture to the rooftop of my apartment building to check out the rally and finish my second cup of coffee. The rally stage was visible as it was south facing near the Washington Monument. Granted it was still rather early, but the famed Trump-campaign playlist of songs like Lee Greenwood's "God Bless the USA" and Laura Branigan's 1980s hit "Gloria" was already on repeat, and people were already trickling in.

After a few minutes of standing in the frigid winter weather, I went back to my apartment to get on with the workday. I wasn't scheduled to head into work until later that afternoon due to COVID-19 risk mitigation efforts, so like I did nearly every day during the pandemic, I killed a couple hours flipping through a rotation of cables news networks and the occasional episode of *It's Always Sunny in Philadelphia*.

Every so often the news would cut from their steady stream of repeated stories over to the rally, and I was able to see clips of the "Trump World" celebrities as they delivered their greatest one-liners, and back and forth. However, one speaker and his comments certainly caught me off guard. Unfortunately, the ramblings of a stolen election, voter fraud, and other conspiracy theories had become commonplace and barely elicited a reaction from me. But one declarative statement made me pause and take immediate notice.

> "If we are wrong, we will be made fools of, but if we're right, a lot of them will go to jail. So, let's have trial by combat!" – Rudy Giuliani, January 6, 2021

Rudy Giuliani, the one-time hero of New York City who captured our hearts as America's mayor, had surely fallen from grace in recent years, but this was different. There was an article in *Foreign Policy* by Caroline O'Hare, printed back in 2007, that called Giuliani a "delusional narcissist," and that was well before the Four Seasons landscaping press conference catastrophe. But something here was different.

Within the crowds of DC, there were always sightings of Giuliani, America's Mayor, whether at the Trump Hotel, Cafe Milano in Georgetown, or a host of other "see and be seen" establishments. It is an interesting life journey for a once-lauded United States attorney, turned reputable mayor, turned "delusional narcissist," then full blown sycophant. And here he is, in front of what is now thousands of supporters of President Donald J. Trump, advocating for the crowd to conduct a "trial by combat." Giuliani would later defend the comments by saying they were hyperbole, that they were a reference to the HBO series *Game of Thrones*, and no reasonable person should have taken them literally. But for the tens of thousands of people in front of him, including the disgraced former law professor John Eastman, who cackled and cheered in approval on stage next to him, the message was clearly received.

In the days preceding the rally, my phone had been constantly going off with Dataminr "hits." Dataminr is an open-source application that uses a propriety algorithm to "scrape" news sites, social media, and other open-source applications and sends alerts about current events, items of interest, and significant activity (SIGACTs). These alerts can be anything from a reported house fire down the street to an insurgent attack in a foreign country. And while I usually dismiss most of the "hits" with an "oh, that's interesting," following the previous right-wing violence in DC from November and December, my ears always perked up whenever I saw anything remotely related to political violence or right-wing extremism.

Like clockwork, when Rudy uttered the provocative statement, Dataminr hits began to light up my phone. It could be complete coincidence, and I'm not one to say that there is any correlation, but after Giuliani's comments, it seemed as if the gates of hell opened. And that's when the news coverage across all cable news channels began to turn to the events in DC. At some point President Trump came to the podium and spoke for about an hour and a half, and I remember watching when he said that he was going to walk with the supporters to the Capitol. It made me think back to an episode of *The West Wing* when Bartlet walks to Capitol Hill, but then I snapped back to reality and said to myself, "There's no way Trump will walk…" both physically and logistically speaking.

By the time President Trump finished his speech, which was approximately seventy minutes in total, ending seemingly off script from his usual "Make America Great Again" stump speech that includes his signature "we will make America strong again, safe again, and great again" catchphrase, hordes of the assembled right-wing extremist groups had already gathered and begun to assault the outer perimeter of the Capitol.

I watched the television as on-the-ground reporters and news organizations scrambled to get handheld cameras up to Capitol Hill and then watched in real time—as did America—as members of the Capitol Police pushed back against a much larger number of protestors. I raced back up to my apartment building rooftop and saw the large mass of people now moving from the Washington Monument eastward, along National Mall, toward the Capitol. There's a scene in the movie *Jaws* when the crew aboard the shark-hunting boat aptly named *Orca* sees the shark for the first time, and the salty Captain Quint remarks, "You're going to need a bigger boat." That was the same sentiment I had in seeing what was unfolding right before my eyes.

I am in no way a psychologist or a social scientist, however, I am familiar with and have read on various theories of crowd dynamics, otherwise known as "mob mentality," which is another reason why my testimony regarding the events at Lafayette Square should have been much more impactful. A French doctor and social psychologist named Gustave Le Bon, considered the pioneer of this field, details this in his seminal work *The Crowd: A Study of the Popular Mind*, which is regarded as the premier piece examining how crowds form and attempting to explain the actions of those involved.

> "It is crowds rather than isolated individuals that may be induced to run the risk of death to secure the triumph of a creed or an idea, that may be fired with enthusiasm for glory and honor... Such heroism is without doubt somewhat unconscious..." – Gustave Le Bon, *The Crowd: A Study of the Popular Mind*, 1895

While Le Bon uses the term "honor" and "heroism," it's important to note that these notions are relative to the people in these crowds. Le Bon also contends that when an individual becomes part of a crowd, that individual undergoes a psychological transformation and acts in accordance with his theory of contagion. The contagion theory states that crowds cause individuals to act in certain ways, and in many cases do things that they as individuals would never do. It, the crowd, the feeling of belonging, and the sense of acting on behalf of something bigger than oneself reference a sort of hypnosis that occurs to individuals within a crowd and alludes to the transformation as being the action of a contagion taking over the individual. This sentiment then spreads throughout the crowd and becomes contagious, and ultimately dangerous. In essence, crowds become mobs because the people within them feel a euphoric sense of invincibility and zero culpability, which then leads to riots and eventually violence.

As the initial wave of insurrectionists fought with the front line of Capitol Police on the west facade facing the National Mall, and the thousands of Trump supporters walked down Constitution Avenue like he ordered them to, according to Le Bon's theory, contagion quickly spread across the hearts and minds of those supporters there to "stop the steal." It was immediately apparent that this situation was quickly escalating out of control. As the supporters merged with the insurrectionists, the contagion quickly enveloped the crowd, and now they were climbing up the facade, scaling the walls, busting barricades, and smashing the windows of the "People's House."

As the scenes at the Capitol became more chaotic, I saw a photo from a Dataminr hit that was posted on social media. It was a fully constructed wooden gallows, on the National Mall, in the shadow of the United States Capitol. Thinking about that now gives me chills. I began texting soldiers in my unit and soldiers in other units, trying to find out if anyone had any information or if they had heard of a recall notice or immediate emergency mobilization. And nearly to a person, the answer was "I got nothing."

Meanwhile, as the United States Senate began their electoral duty of certifying the election, the threat to the United States Congress became too great, and when the insurrectionists breached the last line of defenses and entered the hallowed senate chambers, the various security details assigned to key leaders ushered the 535 members of the senate, and their staffs, to safety. As CNN replayed repeatedly the footage of insurrectionists running up the steps, announcing that the vice president had been ushered out of the senate, I had a sickening feeling. I knew that we, I, should be there. Our Capitol, and capital, needed us.

I still hadn't received any information on a recall or a mobilization for the DCNG under an immediate response authority, but I knew it was just a matter of time. I called into my civilian work and asked them if they were tracking the current situation at the Capitol, and if not, to go to a tv and turn on the news, any news, any channel. On the other end of the phone, I heard a "Holy shit!"

"Yeah, so I won't be coming in today," I told them. My heart began to race a little faster. I then went and grabbed my kit from my storage closet, the same ballistic vest and helmet I had last worn on June 1, and ensured that I had everything I might need on it, which wasn't much—gloves, individual first aid kit (IFAK), a flashlight, a knife, and an emergency tin of Copenhagen tobacco—a standard packing list for all nonstandard missions.

The news became more frantic, and the sense of distress was palpable. I received a text message from a friend who lives on Capitol Hill simply asking, "Where the $@*% are you guys?!" I sent her a note back trying to calm her fears and assuage her concerns, but she was right. Where were we?

Almost as if in a tragicomedy, the news banner then came across the tv screen saying the deployment of the "DC National Guard had been disapproved and denied." My phone began buzzing, ringing, vibrating, and making noises I didn't even know were possible. And it was around that time that I heard the first open-source reports of shots being fired in the Capitol.

I really don't remember how long it took, when the notification was sent, or when I received it, but at some point, I was at the DC Armory. By then the totality of what was occurring hit me. To get to the Armory, which normally would have taken me five minutes, I usually drove eastbound on Constitution Avenue. But I knew that while the roads were probably not closed, they were mobbed by fanatics ransacking the Capitol, so I took the longer route.

The United States Army uses a planning framework called the "Military Decision-Making Process" (MDMP). It is essentially a template for how to analyze, plan, assess, and execute an offensive, defensive, or stability and support operations. One of the key inputs to MDMP is what's called "intelligence preparation of the battlefield" (IPB). IPB is a way to define and assess key factors of an operational area and their effects on our planned operations. The first piece of IPB is to define the operational environment—which includes everything from the terrain to the threats. So, as I sat on the bleachers of the drill floor waiting for orders, I began conducting a hasty MDMP in my head. And first, I tried to define the "threat."

Since that day there has been a lot of talk about how to classify the day, and how to refer to the people who took part. Are they terrorists? Insurgents? There are a lot of nuances to this, but for all intents and purposes—and simplicity's sake—using the Cambridge Dictionary, an insurrection can be defined as an "organized attempt by a group of people to defeat their government and take control of their country." Meanwhile, the same source defines terrorism as "violent action for political purpose." It's a bit of a gray area and certainly one that people will continue to debate, but based on my academic studies and professional work, those people who were now marching through the United States Capitol, defacing the walls with feces, defiling the sacred chambers of democracy, and engaging in hand-to-hand combat with law enforcement, surely, by definition, were insurrectionists. This was an insurrection.

As I continued to do this mission analysis while sitting in the bleachers, more soldiers began trickling in. By this time, the situation looked as if the Capitol had been retaken—but this was only from what I could gather through social media feeds. Around this same time, the DC National Guard Quick Response Force (QRF) deployed from the Armory to the Capitol and supported law enforcement in establishing and securing the perimeter. Then reports came out that pipe bombs had been found at two locations: the Democratic and Republican national committees.

As quickly as the insurrection started, it seemed to eerily dissipate. But that was only because time seemed like a vacuum. The time from the breach to the clearing of the Capitol will forever be five of the darkest hours in American history.

Around 6 p.m. that evening, word was beginning to spread that the United States Congress was going to reconvene and continue their constitutional duty for the electoral certification. It was also at this same time that the magnitude of injuries sustained both by Capitol Police and DC MPD began to surface. Early reports coming in described a hellish scene—one that would only truly come to light in the aftermath of that day. The images of the hand-to-hand combat on the western side of the Capitol can only be described as medieval. Police officers like Michael Fanone being savagely beaten with pipes, tased, and then threatened to be shot with his own weapon. Other officers being assaulted with poles, at the end of which were American flags.

There is very little training anyone can do to prepare themselves for the long-sustained hand-to-hand combat that both the Capitol Police and DC MPD officers endured that day. They were the front and last line of defense against an overwhelming force of insurrectionists. As more of our soldiers came into the Armory and we began to organize, there was a tenseness about what was happening. Nearly all of us had been present at Lafayette Square, but this was completely different. The very essence of our Constitutional Republic was attacked, and the Citadel of Democracy was sacked, right in front of us, as we helplessly watched.

I took the soldiers assigned to my unit aside and talked to them, wanting to check on them. Our small unit was at Lafayette Square, but I wanted to make perfectly clear to them that this was completely different. Whether they agreed with what occurred back in June or not, or whether they supported my actions or not, everyone knew that this was the closest America has come to being overthrown. While we had been activated, we hadn't received any specific marching orders, but it looked like we would be first on mission the following morning. It was nearly midnight now, and I dismissed our soldiers with reporting instructions to arrive back at the Armory at 0500, January 7.

By the time I was driving home, amid the curfew imposed by DC's mayor, Muriel Bowser, Capitol Hill began to resemble the "green zone" in Baghdad. There were checkpoints nearly every block, road closures, blocking positions, and barriers everywhere. Each time I pulled up to an intersection, the authorities manning the post looked at me with a critical consternation. I was wearing my uniform and had my ballistic vest on my passenger seat. Any other day this wouldn't have raised a flag but given that many of the insurrectionists took to wearing military-standard gear and uniforms, and that this wasn't any other day, the authorities were right to be cautious of everyone.

Arriving home that evening, I took my dog, George, for a short walk. From the lobby of my building and the small park out front, I had a perfect view of the Capitol. Underneath the fifteen-thousand-pound Statue of Freedom that adorns the top of the Capitol's dome, the rotunda was still lit. Damaged and fractured, the Capitol still stood like a lighthouse for the "City on a Shining Hill." I took a photo that evening and posted it to Instagram with the caption:

> "The light of democracy, like a lighthouse, may flicker from time to time. And, like a lighthouse, it takes a lightship, a guardian, to ensure that it continues to be and serves as a guiding beacon for liberty and justice."

The next morning, it felt as if the world had been turned upside down. It was very reminiscent of the feelings that I had the morning of September 12, 2001.

Arriving at the Armory, our unit quickly formed up, and then we headed out to the Capitol to relieve some of the forces that had been there all night. Our unit took the south side of Capitol, facing the House of Representatives. We stood watch as the same non-scalable fence from Lafayette Square was installed along the outer perimeter. During the day, I could see members of Congress surveying the damage, both inside and outside the Capitol. Capitol Police, along with other agencies, conducted secondary and tertiary sweeps of the grounds for anything suspicious that may have been placed, such as IEDs or other explosives.

Once we established our perimeter and relieved the outgoing unit, I went inside the Capitol to survey the damage with another member of our unit, Captain Brian White. There was broken glass everywhere as nearly every window had been shattered, and the stains of tear gas and marks of pepper balls served as a reminder of the chaos that occurred only twelve hours earlier. Captain White and I conducted an informal site survey to try to understand how this attack occurred and unfolded. It became quickly apparent that the insurrectionists came from nearly all sides of the Capitol. Some were able to come up from the west, others from the east, and then some even scaled the walls of the north to enter. They had not only overwhelmed the Capitol but also isolated it. It was, from my perspective, a well-organized and planned assault.

I traced the footsteps of Capitol Police Officer Eugene Goodman, who selflessly and heroically led the insurrectionists away from the chambers and prevented what would have undoubtedly led to an assassination of a sitting member of Congress. The closed-circuit television footage of his actions is harrowing and terrifying. It's a credit to the Capitol Police and the DC MPD that not one member of the United States Congress, nor their staff, was injured that day.

Captain White and I, still surveying the damage, then ran into a young Capitol Police officer. He looked exhausted. We exchanged some pleasantries, and then I asked him how he was doing. If there's one thing a combat veteran knows, it's the look of the "thousand-yard stare." This young officer, a kid, had just gone to hell and back. So, while he responded to my initial question with a nonchalant remark, I then asked him a bit more pointedly, "Are you doing alright?"

It's interesting how rephrasing a question, putting a certain emphasis on a key word, or even simply changing a tone of voice can make all the difference, because when I asked him that question, he must have realized that I wasn't asking about him as an officer, but as a person, and the flood gates opened. He began to tell me how quickly it all happened. He explained how he was manning his post inside the Capitol when suddenly, they were overrun on all sides. He told me about how they expended all their riot control agents and pepper balls and literally thought that they might die there at the hands of their own fellow Americans. He explained how they had no idea how many insurrectionists there were but only knew that they were vastly outnumbered. And with a glisten in his eye, he simply asked me, "Where were you guys?"

Later that night, only twenty-four hours since the insurrectionists desecrated the Citadel of Democracy, I was standing in the freezing winter cold when a young congressional staffer invited me and Captain White to their office for some hot coffee and tea. We had been manning the perimeter since early in the morning, and heat and caffeine were in short supply, and we weren't sure when we would be relieved.

Walking into the maze that is the Longworth office building, ironically the same one where I testified the previous summer, we found the office that the nice young lady invited us to. I should have known from their hospitality that she, and the representative she worked for, were from Texas. We proceeded to talk with the staffers and ask how they were handling everything, and if they were all right. A couple of them expressed grave fears while some others were rather dismissive about the events of the previous day. I tried my best not to tip my hand as to who I was, a failed political hack and tarnished whistleblower, but found it fascinating to get their perspective on the events.

They asked some questions about the security operations and

what our mission was, but I didn't want to give them too many details. On one hand, I'm always concerned about operational security (OPSEC), and on the other, I truthfully had no idea what was going on in the big picture. The dust hadn't even settled yet, threats were still coming in, and we all knew that extremists were still out there, so we were there until we were relieved.

Then I told the staffers about the conversation I had hours earlier with the young Capitol Police officer. I gave them a summary of his remarks but then looked them, the staffers, dead in the eyes and said, "These guys are going to need a lot of mental health and emotional support." That was not what the staffers expected me to say. They were kind of taken aback by my comment but intrigued as to what I meant by it. I explained, "Look, it's one thing to loot and burn a convenience store. But when you're engaged in hand-to-hand combat, fighting for what you believe is the very essence of American democracy and your life, that's a much different and much more traumatizing event than seeing a 7-11 looted."

At that moment, the congressman, Representative Jodey Arrington (R-TX), walked in. A tall Texan with a thick West Texas accent. We exchanged pleasantries, and I thanked him for his staff's hospitality. And as I was getting ready to bid the staff farewell, one of his aides said, "Sir, can you tell him what you said?"

I replied, "About what?"

She then insisted, "About the mental health support stuff you talked about."

With this proverbial door wide open, I retold the story of the young Capitol Police officer to the congressman with greater emphasis and detail than before to relay the concern and urgency of the situation. Despite using all the persuasive techniques I could conjure, it seemingly fell on deaf ears. His response was something to the effect of how the insurrectionists didn't topple or destroy any of the statues in Statuary Hall, so it must not have been that bad. This sentiment was later disingenuously echoed by countless Republican members of Congress who stated that the insurrectionists inside the Capitol were merely "tourists."

Leaving Rep. Arrington's office that night, the night after an insurrection in the United States Capitol, I felt the same grief-stricken anger I felt in the days after Lafayette Square. Did we not see the same thing? Are we so divided as a country that we see two different truths because of our political ideologies? To be clear, and in a nod to those brave journalists who withstood threats and assaults that day, video footage they captured definitively shows insurrectionists beating law enforcement officers with an American flag. That's not a deep state, deep fake video, or some up-down-left-right propaganda; that happened, that actually happened. And there are countless other stories like that.

As Captain White and I walked back out to the perimeter through one of the tunnels underneath the Capitol, still reeling from the dumbfounding conversation we just had, the first report came in. Capitol Police Officer Brian Sicknick had passed away. We didn't know the background or the story of what happened or how he died, but immediately the grief across the Capitol complex and among the Capitol Police was palpable. I gathered some of our soldiers that were with us and let them know of the report. They reacted just like I expected, as if we had lost one of our own.

I gave my sympathies to the Capitol Police officers standing watch with us and reaffirmed my personal support for them, both as guardians on the watch, and as human beings. I knew that the toughest days were still ahead. Tragically, the same warning I gave to Rep. Arrington materialized. Because a few days later, veteran Capitol Police Officer Howard Liebengood, who had served since

2005, committed suicide.

Later that night going into the morning of January 8, we continued to receive threats of violence from open source and reports from both the Secret Service and FBI field office. One such report was of a possible vehicle-borne improvised explosive device (VBIED). The report had such specificity that it had the name of the person of interest and the exact vehicle that this was going to be in.

Quickly, our forces along with Capitol Police "buttoned up" the perimeter, meaning that we closed all the fortified gates and moved out teams away from the fence line. Meanwhile, Capitol Police began issuing out "long guns"—AR15s—to their officers present, as FBI and emergency response teams (ERT) began patrolling up and down Constitution and Independence Avenues. Tensions were extremely high, and rightfully so. Thankfully, the threat was mitigated, but once the all clear was given, I walked inside the Capitol. It had now been nearly thirty-six hours since the insurrection. I walked through the halls, and it was at this point that the totality of everything, everything that happened, and everything that was to come came full circle. I was standing in the middle of the Capitol rotunda, exhausted, questioning everything.

Why did this all happen? Could this have been prevented? What happens next? Is this the new normal for America? These were all questions that I think everyone across the country was asking. Sitting in silence on one of the benches, I lay down and tried to get some sleep. But I had one very personal question, one that I still battle with to this day. Was this my fault?

It seems foolish, but given all that had happened over the course of the six months leading up to this moment, I couldn't help but think that my own personal actions may have contributed to this. Had I not stood up and forward about what occurred that past

June, would the DCNG have been fully activated earlier? Was it because of my testimony that leaders across the Department of Defense were concerned about the political optics of uniformed military members around the Capitol? There were a million "what if" scenarios running through my head, but as I opened my eyes one last time, lying on this creaky old bench in the still brightly lit rotunda, under the watchful eye of *The Apotheosis of Washington*, a fresco I had stared up at numerous times, I saw something different. I had never noticed this before, but that night, fading underneath where George Washington sits was a rainbow. Its colors faded since it was finished in 1865, ironically the year the Civil War ended, and I remembered back to the old saying that "after a storm there's a rainbow."

As I closed my eyes in the Capitol Rotunda, steps away from where the likes of Presidents Lincoln and Kennedy, Senator McCain, Representative Lewis, and countless other American heroes had lain in state, I prayed for a rainbow. A new chapter after some of the darkest days in American history.

Chapter 21

THE FALL OF KABUL

In 1962, General Douglas MacArthur, one of the most famed West Point graduates, gave an address to the United States Corps of Cadets that instantly became one of the most important and most often referenced speeches given at the Academy.

> "The Long Gray Line has never failed us. Were you to do so, a million ghosts in olive drab, in brown khaki, in blue and gray, would rise from their white crosses, thundering those magic words: Duty, Honor, Country." – General Douglas MacArthur

On August 16, 2021, I watched from the study of my house on Capitol Hill in horror as footage began circulating showing hundreds and thousands of Afghans overrunning Hamid Karzai International Airport (HKIA). The footage of Afghans clinging to the wheel wells of a C-17 Globemaster as it took off and then falling to their deaths was one that forever will be—and should be—imprinted in my mind.

I was keenly aware of the dire security situation as I had been closely following the Taliban advance toward Kabul during the summer of 2021. And as soon as the open-source reports said that

President Ghani had fled the country, I knew that the country had failed and fallen. I can't really remember how things got started in those early days, but as the world watched with collective despair, I was contacted by a fellow West Point graduate who asked if I had any contacts on the ground there at HKIA. I had never deployed to Afghanistan, not that I didn't want to, but the opportunity just never presented itself, which is ironic as it was the longest war in US history. But given my ties in and around the Department of Defense, the national security sector, and well, nearly all of Washington, DC, he thought I might know someone or anyone that could assist in what was a life-or-death situation. The situation, I would learn, was that he was in contact with several West Point graduates who were Afghan citizens and either active or former military officers.

West Point has a long history of bringing foreign nationals to the Academy where they study, live, train, and then graduate to go on and serve their home countries in their home militaries. This program not only builds great leaders for foreign militaries, but also helps drive security cooperation between the United States and those countries. But there's also a downside. And that is, if something occurs, whether a civil war, a coup d'état, or in this case a completely fallen country, those same Cadets turned graduates then become some of the highest value targets for the enemy. Because not only are they trained and educated, but they did so with and through the United States. And in this specific instance, where the Taliban, our sworn enemy, were knocking through the gates of Kabul, the capital of Afghanistan, it was only a matter of time before our guys and their families were found and executed.

What happened next has been referred to as the "Digital Dunkirk," an ode to the 1940 mass evacuation of hundreds of thousands of British soldiers across the English Channel in what was called Operation Dynamo. But instead of using fishing boats to ferry people across the cold choppy waters from France to England, the "lifeboats" in this instance were cell phones. Individual text messages from one person to another became group chats, which then became WhatsApp and Signal groups, with hundreds of messages began being sent, to mobilize thousands of people across the world to help save the lives of Americans and our allies now trapped behind enemy lines.

Over the next twelve to twenty-four hours, for the ad hoc "West Point Evacuation Group," our primary focus was on getting the West Point guys out. While they were Afghan citizens, to us they were our brothers in arms. In these groups and chats, we immediately mobilized and began assuming roles that we had had during our time in service. Military intelligence officers began tracking open-source reports and developing common intelligence pictures. Logistics planners began looking at various logistical routes and locations for medical supplies, food, and water. Operational enablers began setting up tactics, techniques, and procedures to get our guys noticed at the gates by US military forces. It was quite extraordinary how quickly this occurred as this twenty-first century Digital Dunkirk took shape, through the passionate compassion of hundreds and thousands of military veterans and everyday civilians.

Through our collective networks, namely the Long Gray Line, we had been able to get in contact with several soldiers who were manning the gates, standing guard in the face of tens of thousands of desperate Afghans trying to flee for their lives. This was both highly unusual and highly, highly dangerous as it jeopardized the safety of not only our West Point guys but also the safety of those service members guarding HKIA. So, while parts of our group continued to have direct talks with the West Point guys, others were working the phones, reaching out to anyone we knew in the Army, Marine Corps, Air Force, US Central Command, hell, the entire Department of Defense. We were in a race against time to get these guys, our guys, through the crowds and mobs and to safety.

As we were trying to find ways to get our guys to the gate and into the haven that had become the HKIA flight line, one of our guys ("Nick") was sharing photos and videos from the chaos that was ensuing just beyond the fortified walls lined with concertina (barbed) wire. Images of Taliban fighters patrolling the crowds carrying AK-47s and US-made M4 rifles and M249 squad automatic weapons caused massive panic and surges at the gates, along with providing real-time proof of the imminent threats. And if that wasn't enough to galvanize our efforts, we were also working against the self-imposed deadline of August 31.

In April 2021 President Biden and his administration declared that by September 11, 2021, all US forces would be out of Afghanistan. But then on July 9, 2021, President Biden announced that that deadline would be moved up, to August 31. The domino effect of this steadfast proclamation was that as the Taliban was already picking up momentum in the south and east of Afghanistan, now the US was in a time constraint to get thousands of troops back to the United States along with billions of dollars' worth of equipment and vehicles as well. The equipment that couldn't be redeployed in time would be "de-militarized," meaning destroyed, and then left for whoever came upon it. And now Kabul, the last remaining installation under US control, the last US bastion after twenty years of war in Afghanistan, was the only hope left for thousands of Americans and American allies who were left in Afghanistan.

Our group continued to use any angle, use any leverage,

and call in any favor we could to get the attention of someone important who could help us get these West Point graduates to safety. We scrolled through social media feeds looking for contact information for senior government officials and searched through years' worth of email traffic to find the contact information for that one person who with the push of a button could help us. There had to be someone who would help us.

Years earlier I had a random and brief email exchange with General David Petraeus, a West Point graduate and the former commander of the 101st Airborne Division, the Multi-National Force Iraq, CENTCOM, NATO International Security Force Assistance (ISAF) in Afghanistan, and the former the director at the Central Intelligence Agency under President Obama. He was the guy we needed. So, I dropped back and threw up what was a two-minute drill "Hail Mary," knowing that this would, like most two-minute drills, end with an anticlimactic blow of the whistle ending the game. Except this wasn't a game, this was the lives of our guys hanging in the balance. I thought to myself, "$@*% it," hit send, and waited.

Not more than five minutes went by before I got a response. The young kid in me who admired General Petraeus was a bit starstruck at first, but I didn't have time to waste. We immediately began sending messages back and forth, and I quickly realized that he was immediately invested in this sensitive operation to rescue our West Point team. He then began putting me in touch with other people who were doing the same thing. He was the guy. He began advising me on other considerations and sent over some ideas for tactics and techniques to get our team not only to but through the gates.

Because of General Petraeus, our informal networks began to coalesce, and the demand for support surged exponentially. While the primary focus for our ad hoc team was and continued to be our West Point guys, I was soon working with some of his contacts to assist in moving other people around Kabul, getting them to the right gates, the right locations, and hoping that we could get them into HKIA. As this demand continued to exponentially surge, in the back of my mind I knew that we would be in this for a while, and I was in it for the long haul.

A day or two into this ordeal—time feels like it didn't exist as I was running on pizza delivery and carrot cake—and after numerous, more like hundreds, of very frank and matter of fact conversations with people at HKIA, members of our team stateside were able to formulate a plan to get our guys to the gates and to safety. To say how they got into the gates of HKIA isn't necessarily my story to tell. But the harrowing minutes—which went by like hours—as we watched and waited for updates from them as they pushed their way to the front of the mobs and were essentially extracted from the crowds by heroic US military service members is a night I will never forget. It wasn't until early the next morning—I can't remember which day it was at this point—that we received the message and photo we all had been waiting for. It was confirmation that "Nick" was inside HKIA with his family and our team.

"Nick," the team, and their families were almost immediately loaded onto a C-17 and headed off to a safe location. My mom had been aware of what was occurring and what our little group was doing, so as I still do whenever something good happens in my life, I sent her a text message saying, "we got them," and immediately followed it up with an early morning phone call, which resulted in me essentially breaking down in tears of joy and exhaustion. When word got out across the West Point community that "Nick" and the guys got out, there was near jubilation across social media.

And while it was a small victory in what was a pending massive defeat, it was a monumental victory nonetheless.

I then emailed my "newfound advisor" and recent "pen pal," General Petraeus, to give him an update on the situation. It was a quick email, thanking him for his assistance and letting him know that "Nick" and the West Point guys and their families were safe and off to an undisclosed location. He immediately replied, giving the little kid in me affirmation from one of the highest military leaders of my generation, and congratulated our efforts. Then with the cool demeanor that only someone who has led some of the largest operations of the twenty-first century could have, in an indirect but implied way, he gave me my next order: "Scale it."

Our group that had organized and orchestrated this movement had grown significantly since August 16, and we all knew that the situation was only worsening hour by hour. And as much as we all wanted to take a break, nap, and crack open a beer, General Petraeus was right. We had a successfully proven operation, and we all inherently knew we couldn't stop now. It was time to scale. Utilizing our military knowledge and collective professional civilian experience, our group set up a de facto case management system to get Afghan allies' information where we could then triage specific "cases"—people—and formalize a process for each of us to individually reach out, advise, guide, and counsel Afghan allies' as to where to go, what to do, and how to get there. What started out as a few dozen names quickly became an exponentially growing list. And over the course of one week, it grew to over 50,000 Afghan allies and their families seeking to flee the Taliban. And it was at that point that Allied Airlift was established.

Allied Airlift 21 (AA21) was a hasty nonprofit that we set up to mitigate liability but also to organize our efforts in working with the Department of Defense. We understood that they were the ones in harm's way, they were the ones calling the shots, and they were the ones doing the Lord's work. We were there to support them in any way we could, as force multipliers, and to enable their operations to safely evacuate as many Afghan allies as possible in what was one of if not the largest non-combat evacuation in modern history.

As our organization grew, our information spread, and intake into our database surged, I received a call from a dear friend—and old boss—who now worked on Capitol Hill. Will Johnson was my former battalion commander from Fort Hood after coming home from Iraq in 2011 when I was at my personal low point and at my professional worst. He's a great guy and even greater leader, and someone who rightfully and probably should have despised me. But instead, over the course of 2020 and 2021, he had reached out to see how I was doing given all the trouble that I had been part of, involved with, and witness to. But this time, he was calling to see if I could help him with an issue. He had a task he needed assistance with. I immediately transported back to the spring 2012, when I was a lieutenant in the 5th Battalion, 82nd Field Artillery Regiment, and I was receiving a mission from my battalion commander. And this time I wasn't going to let him down.

Will, formerly call sign "Black Dragon 6," then put me in contact with former Congressman Tom Suozzi (D-NY). Tom was contacted by a constituent of his named Mohammed Wali, who was an American citizen. Mohammed's wife, Aishah, and two young children were back in Afghanistan visiting family in the summer of 2021 when the Taliban began their path of destruction to Kabul. And now, they were one of the thousands of Americans, nevertheless tens of thousands of Afghan allies, desperately seeking a way out. And Mohammed was helpless as he watched Kabul fall thousands of miles away, knowing his family was there in the middle of it all.

Aishah and her children had gone to the gates at HKIA several times over the course of several days but could never get close enough to be noticed by the gate guards. Even as they frantically held up their blue American passports. By this point, the newly formed AA21 had a pretty good system working, and we had established connections to people on the ground outside of HKIA—"fixers"—who began to help us run operations. These fixers would pick up people and quickly move them to other locations where they would rendezvous with American forces who were opening different gates at different times at different locations. It was a giant game of coordinated whack-a-mole.

I explained the situation on the ground and how AA21 operated, and I advised him that, because it was such a dynamically dangerous situation, I couldn't make any promises. Tom, with the confidence that only a Congressman from New York could have, brushed that all aside and made it known that he knew we would get this done—part inspirational, part threatening, as only a New Yorker could do.

He then connected me to one of his young staffers, Caroline Cosgrove. Caroline was in direct contact with the Wali family—both Mohammed in the States and Aishah in Afghanistan—and was serving as both constituent liaison to Mohammed and grief counselor to Aishah. I briefed Caroline on the ground situation, how we operated, and how this extraction would unfold. I also gave her the same disclaimer that I gave her boss, Tom. I couldn't make any promises. Caroline, also from New York, took it the same way he did.

Caroline briefed me up on Aishah and explained that she was with her younger brother, Nassir. And while Nassir was barely eighteen years old, he wasn't an American citizen and didn't have a visa on hand. He had applied through the Special Immigrant Visa (SIV) program but had no paperwork or confirmation that it was accepted. There are numerous failures that occurred to allow the situation in Afghanistan to deteriorate as fast as it did, but the one overarching failure of the United States Government was the absolute dumpster fire that was the SIV program. Nassir was unfortunately just another statistic lost in the bureaucratic SIV shitshow.

Caroline then connected me to the Aishah, and we began a group chat to begin the coordination for a rendezvous and pick up. I wanted to ensure that they were prepared for the uncertainty that was about to unfold, and given that one of the children was a young infant, the military planner in me was extremely concerned about the high heats of summer and the potential for dehydration. There would be no food, no water, and no shelter, and Aishah and the children needed to be prepared to endure hours of being in the sun. Furthermore, I told them that they could only bring one bag, which they would have to be able to hand carry. With these limitations and restrictions, the dark truth in the back of my mind was that if Taliban bullets didn't kill them, the elements could. Then the next shoe dropped.

I explained to Aishah how this operation would work. Basically, she would go to a location that I would provide and wait to be picked up by a local national who would then take her and the children to an undisclosed safe house where they would then wait longer until given the word to go to the extraction point back at HKIA. To add onto the difficulties of the situation, the graveness of the circumstances, and the dire reality of what was occurring, Aishah's English wasn't that good. So that added another layer of complexity to this entire operation as I tried to assuage her fears that this was how we were going to get her to safety.

After a couple of hours of planning internally with our teams and the constant back and forth of trying to convince Aishah of this course of action, I got word that the pick-up was ready to move. It was time to go. But before Aisha left the house for the last time, I asked her to put something identifiable on the baby. Doing so would help distinguish them from the thousands of people and help our "guy" find them quickly and begin the extraction. Aishah complied, and tied a red bandana around the baby, and left the house through Taliban checkpoints toward Abbey Gate.

Before this operation even had the chance to fail, it was already almost over. The mission was seemingly lost in translation, because when Aishah got to the location near Abbey Gate, which was a very specific street corner, she saw that there was no escort waiting on them. So, they began to turn around and return home, figuring that this was another failed attempt to get to safety.

Caroline frantically tried to calm them down and assure Aishah that this indeed was part of the plan, and that they needed to stay out for however long it took. Caroline, who normally worked basic constituent services and had never served in the military let alone coordinated rather covert extractions, became a huge asset as she could assuage their fears in a way that only a woman could do for another woman. And truthfully, had Caroline not been able to do that, and had Aishah turned back just then, they would probably still be in Afghanistan today, or worse.

It's human nature that when doing these cloak-and-dagger-esque extractions from thousands of miles away to want updates every minute on the minute. But the reality is, that's not how it works. Hours went by without updates. Caroline and I stayed in contact, but there was nothing I could provide. The team had positive control of the targets, and we had to exercise tactical patience while they executed the operation. But try explaining that to a young congressional staffer from New York, or better yet her boss from New York.

With no updates over the course of several hours, Tom called over to Will to tell him that the mission was a failure—and that I had gone dark on them. But the truth was, we needed time even as we knew that time was our enemy. It's hard to explain that to anyone, let alone a sitting member of the United States Congress, but we weren't in charge, and we could only get the ball to the one-yard line. It was up to a team of heroic individuals in the middle of hell on earth to punch it in to the endzone.

After sitting on an idle chat nearly all night, and by now four days into this specific extraction, I received word that under the cover of darkness, the Wali family was extracted from the city and was safely in HKIA awaiting transport aboard a C-17. Another small win.

When I received word through our back channels, I contacted the family and had them send a photo from inside the gate—trust but verify—which I then forwarded to Tom and Will to notify them that the Wali family was safe. I signed off that email with the succinct message of "God Bless America." But there was one problem with the photo, the brother, Nassir, wasn't in it.

Nassir, without a green card, and no passport—because his passport was at the US Embassy, which was overrun and looted—or any other type of documents, couldn't go with the extraction team. He was a tall, shy kid, spoke no English, loved basketball, and now he was left in Afghanistan, alone.

After the Wali extraction, I was contacted numerous times—many times frantically—by people trying to get the sources and methods we had used to get this done. While this "operation" was off the books, unsanctioned, yet seemingly parallel to the largest non-combatant evacuation operation (NEO) in recent history,

I often referenced the story from *Charlie Wilson's War*, where Congressman Wilson was in danger of violating The Logan Act—which criminalizes negotiation by unauthorized American citizens with foreign governments—as he provided resources, support, and funding for the Mujahideen in Afghanistan in the 1980s to fight the Russians. And much like Charlie, this "digital Dunkirk" was very much in the gray area and may have been teetering on the lines of legality. But given that only two people in American history have ever been indicted on these charges—neither convicted—and that our mission was for all intents and purposes righteous and virtuous, I wasn't too worried. Plus, if it ever came to that, Congressman Tom Suozzi assured me that he had my back, just as I had had his.

Chapter 22

A PROMISE

A couple of days later I got a strange call from a man whom I had met years before, David Urban. David, a West Point graduate from the class of 1986, was a guy I was introduced to when I first moved to DC. He was then a lobbyist, having worked on Capitol Hill where he made a name for himself as one of the premier and prominent power players in Congress. He also was a regular contributor on cable news networks but even more notably was a close Trump associate aligned with the now former president. Word somehow got to him about our operations, and he had a case: Huma Aatifi.

Huma was an American citizen who went to college in America, but at the time she was living with her extended family in Afghanistan. When Kabul fell, she had tried to get out several times but had been repeatedly pushed back and beaten both by the Taliban and other Afghans. When David called, and knowing the gravitas that he has, I assumed that Huma had some pull or that there was some association that made her a "high value individual (HVI)." She immediately became my number one priority.

I began speaking directly to Huma along with her American friend Afton Carlson, who was stateside but had been trying to help Huma evacuate for days. Initially, David told me that Huma had a small family with her—totaling approximately four or five people—but by the time I spoke with her, it had grown to twenty people. I could barely get one person out, let alone twenty!

In speaking with Huma, her position was clear. Unless her whole family got out, she wasn't leaving. On the phone with her and Afton numerous times, I tried to make it perfectly clear that I couldn't make any promises. I told her I'd do my best to get everyone out, but there may be a time where she would need to decide whether to leave or to stay, and that decision was hers and hers alone to make.

I knew it would take a couple of days to get Huma and the family out, so I had them stay at their house for the time being. I told them to continue to eat and relax—a very relative term for the given situation—and the time would come when we were ready to move. But then I asked her for a favor. Nassir, the brother from the Wali family, was still in Kabul, so I asked Huma if he could join them. What's one more to a family of twenty? So, I introduced Huma to her "new cousin," Nassir, and he joined them at their safe house a couple of kilometers from Abbey Gate.

Many of the informal groups operating in this "Digital Dunkirk" had been using WhatsApp, and we received word that the Taliban may have been able to infiltrate and compromise the threads. There were numerous reports of Taliban fighters stealing passports and phones from people so in reality, it was only a matter of time before it was all compromised. From an operational security standpoint, nothing was safe. Names, numbers, and locations now all in the hands of the enemy. The entire evacuation of Afghanistan was at risk.

It was at this same time that Huma got a call from someone claiming to be an American who said that she had to go to the airfield immediately. And if she didn't, then the Taliban were coming to get her. The unidentified caller threatened that they knew where she was, and she only had twenty minutes to leave. And only she could go, no one else.

I immediately got a frantic call from her hysterically crying. She had walked up to the roof of the house they were at to process what the unidentified caller had said, and in between her near hyperventilation, I was able to ascertain that someone had called and said she was going to be killed. I had no idea what was happening. But given that all the contacts, names, and numbers had been compromised, I immediately concluded that this was the Taliban. There were reports of the Taliban contacting Afghans saying that they were working with the Americans and would come and pick them up. The Afghans would follow their directions and orders only to be met by the Taliban in the street and then executed.

But that was all stuff that I knew that I hadn't shared with Huma or her friend Afton because, frankly, they had other things to worry about. So now, not only was I dealing with the uncertainty of the extraction, trying to figure out how to get now twenty-one people into HKIA, but I was also having to prove to Huma and Afton that I was who I said I was. Instead of trying to explain my background, give my résumé, or provide a litany of personal and professional references, given my lack of patience, absence of time, and absolute exhaustion, I simply said two words: "Google me."

It only took a minute and Afton began to realize that I could be and was a trusted agent. His assurance then reassured Huma, and not long after we were all back on track, ironically laughing about what almost happened. That is, Huma being lured out to a location, kidnapped, and executed. But as we put the issue aside, and I told Huma to go back downstairs to her family and to relax, I made the biggest mistake anyone in this or any dire situation can ever make. I promised her that I would get her and her family out.

Right when it left my mouth, I knew it was a promise I probably couldn't keep. I immediately regretted it and wished I could retract it with verbal whiteout. But the dye was cast.

I had Huma send me photos of everyone in their family for our teams to be able to recognize them and to later verify identities. I asked her to send me headshots of everyone, but in true to form fashion, instead of stoic poses on a white background, I got what can only be described as a version of Afghan glamour shots. It was a brief moment of levity in a $@*%ing terrible situation. But one photo stood out: Sandara.

With big bulging eyes, a mischievous smile, and a Dora the Explorer haircut, Sandara was two years old and became the face of this mission for me. I don't know what it was or why, but I became fixated on this little girl. An innocent child born into a terrible world, a victim of circumstance, and now potentially a victim of war. As I went through the documents Huma sent me, and began sorting them into our database, for some reason I printed off the photo of Sandara, folded it, and put it in my pocket. I was not going to let her down.

I had been in regular contact with several soldiers during the evacuation. One in particular, an officer from the 10th Mountain Division, who will remain anonymous, had been a great asset in previous operations. But I also knew that as time continued to wind down, and the clock hands inched closer to August 31, he was receiving orders and his focus was now safely getting his soldiers out of Afghanistan. I reached out to him about Huma to see if there was any way we could push through twenty-one people into his secured sector. I knew the answer before I even asked it, and to confirm my suspicions, I was immediately met with not just a no, but a "$@*% no."

Reports began circulating that the Islamic State Khorasan Province (ISIS-K), an offshoot of ISIS and a sworn enemy of both the United States and Taliban, were planning an attack. That very real threat, coupled with the looming deadline, meant that the likelihood of getting Huma, Sandara, and their twenty other family members out, was rapidly declining. They were desperate, and frankly, so was I. I had made a promise that I was going to have to break. I began scribbling some notes as to what to say and how to say it. In all my years, I never got any training on how to tell someone that they were being left behind by their own government and that they needed to hide and barricade themselves in a house, otherwise they'll more than likely be executed.

I reached back out to my contact one last time. I don't know if my desperation came through via text messages, but I was using every lever, tugging on every heart string, and begging to every religious deity, to find some way, somehow to make this extraction happen. And then, my last-ditch effort, I sent him the photo. I prayed that thousands of miles away, a young army officer on the receiving end of that photo would look young Sandara in the eyes and see what I saw.

A minute went by without a response. I stared at the screen, as the lives of twenty-one people and the hopes and dreams of young Sandara hung in the balance, then I saw three dots appear in the chat message: "Be at Black Gate at 0100."

I didn't even have time to thank him, but I immediately called Huma and said, "It's time to move, now!" This was the call Huma and her family had been waiting for. I gave very explicit and matter-of-fact instructions: "no bags, and you have ten minutes to leave." And to her credit, Huma took the orders like a soldier.

By this point, the Taliban had imposed a curfew in Kabul, so telling Huma and her family composed of young women, one cousin who has Down syndrome, her aunt with one leg, and a couple of other young military-aged males—including Nassir from the Wali family—to get their bags—I used much more colorful language at the time—and get to the airfield immediately was a bit of a challenge.

Miraculously, they were able to get four taxis at midnight in the middle of Kabul to drive all of them to this nondescript location that I sent to her on Google Maps. I gave her explicit instructions that they need to get dropped off at one location, and then walk along an unmarked trail to the location of "Black Gate."

Black Gate was a lesser-known gate that was being used sporadically and unofficially. It was a close-hold location that nearly everyone working these evacuation extractions understood to only give out in confidence. Well, that plan was thrown out the window when someone posted on social media the locations of all the entrance control points, access points, and gates at HKIA. With a giant black arrow pointing to the exact location of Black Gate. The secret was out, and our operation was compromised.

Pulling up to Black Gate, and with the location compromised, there were already hundreds of people massing nearby. Huma's group of twenty, plus Nassir, walked the trail and got to the location I had sent. They sent me a photo of where they were so I could verify it and confirm with the US forces on the other side. Except instead of it only being them there, they were surrounded by hundreds of other Afghans.

Murphy's Law says, "everything that can go wrong will go wrong and at the worst possible time." Now I don't know who Murphy is, or how he came up with that saying, or if Murphy is even a real person. But what I do know is that if Murphy is real, and if he did come up with that, then he certainly was from Afghanistan.

Once I verified Huma's location, I contacted another officer who was on the other side of the gate. Receiving the photos I had sent and the updates I had from Huma, he was able to triangulate their specific location and get "eyes on"—confirm their location—from their side of the wall. Everything was in place. One problem though, the crowds continued to grow. And when crowds grow, bad stuff always happens. Whether it's the Taliban shooting into the crowds or the crowds themselves mobbing the gates, large crowds could and would jeopardize the security of HKIA. So, to deter this, soldiers and marines would employ riot control agents (RCAs) to back off or disperse the crowd—tactics I had become intimately familiar with in 2020.

I told Huma that this would happen and, when it does, not to run, but instead and counterintuitively, to move toward the gate. I explained that the gate is going to open, and the soldiers are going to come out and throw some flash bangs to startle and scatter the crowd. At which point, other soldiers are going to come out and physically grab you and bring you into HKIA. So, the explicit task is to not move when it happens, but the implied task is that you need to convince all twenty-one other people to do the same. Her family had to trust her, and she had to trust me.

Then I got word from guys on the other side: they were moving. And like clockwork, and with the precision that only the finest soldiers in the world can have, the gate opened, the lead element deployed the RCAs, and at the same time, another team went and physically grabbed Huma and her group of twenty-one people. And then communications went silent.

Minutes turned to hours. No sign of life from Huma. Thousands of miles away, I paced around in my Capitol Hill row home, waiting for any update.

Adam D. DeMarco

Afton, who was also on the chat, yelled via text, "HUMA!"

Three dots appeared showing she was beginning to type.

She's inside.

I respond, "Confirm again, you have all members and Nassir?"

She responds with an emoji face with a tear.

Afton prods her again. "Do you have everyone, Huma?"

Then one of the best messages I've ever received: "Yesssss."

I then, mentally drained, responded, "For $@*%'s sake—no more jokes!"

And she responded with the best selfie photo I've ever received: her and her family on the tarmac. All twenty-two people in total, scrunched into one dark and blurry picture. And then she sent me one of my most cherished photos to this day, and that was Sandara, peacefully asleep in the arms of her uncle.

Afton sent photos of him and his family sitting together crying on the couch, I sent them a photo back smiling—it was the first time they had seen me. They were finally putting a name to a face, the face of a stranger who just was trying to do the right thing in the worst of circumstances.

Later that day I called David to let him know we got Huma out, along with her entire family including her new cousin Nassir. I then asked him who Huma was. Was she a diplomat? Some Afghan royalty? A friend of President Biden's? An associate of President Trump's?

He paused for a second and then responded, much to my surprise, "Oh, I thought you knew her."

In the end, Huma was just an American woman, trying to do what was best for her family. And it just so happened out of

238

what we can only say is pure luck—or providence—she ended up getting connected to a couple of people who had the means and, most importantly, the willpower to help.

In the days following the successful extraction and evacuation of Huma and her family, I began to wind down my individual involvement in the overarching evacuation. Many more organizations with many more resources began to organize and coalesce and frankly, I was burned out. And with the withdrawal deadline of August 31 fast approaching, I knew that this would be an enduring challenge and best done by supporting those best suited for it. My friends, Nick Palmisciano, another West Point graduate, along with Sarah Verardo, Tim Kennedy, and Chad Robichaux, had recently traveled directly to Afghanistan and were working on the ground at HKIA, doing God's work, with their newly established organization Save Our Allies. Collectively, their group of twelve people directly evacuated over 12,000 people out of Kabul to safety.

A couple of days later, on August 26, the inevitable occurred. Abbey Gate, the site that I sent Aishah to days before, was the target of an attack by ISIS-K. The attack killed thirteen service members and countless civilians. I can't speak to how it occurred, what could have been done to mitigate it, or if this was in any way avoidable, but what I can say is that fully knowing the threat, the thirteen service members who died that day did so while saving lives. They knew the risks to themselves yet continued to do what they could so that others could get to safety. We often hear about people dying as heroes, but we don't often hear about them living as such. And while I never met those brave thirteen service members, I can tell you this: their actions and efforts saved thousands of lives during the evacuation Afghanistan. Those thirteen not only died as heroes, but more importantly, lived as them.

Marine Corps Staff Sgt. Darin T. Hoover, 31,
of Salt Lake City, Utah.

Marine Corps Sgt. Johanny Rosario Pichardo, 25,
of Lawrence, Massachusetts.

Marine Corps Sgt. Nicole L. Gee, 23,
of Sacramento, California.

Marine Corps Cpl. Hunter Lopez, 22,
of Indio, California.

Marine Corps Cpl. Daegan W. Page, 23,
of Omaha, Nebraska.

Marine Corps Cpl. Humberto A. Sanchez, 22,
of Logansport, Indiana.

Marine Corps Lance Cpl. David L. Espinoza, 20,
of Rio Bravo, Texas.

Marine Corps Lance Cpl. Jared M. Schmitz, 20,
of St. Charles, Missouri.

Marine Corps Lance Cpl. Rylee J. McCollum, 20,
of Jackson, Wyoming.

Marine Corps Lance Cpl. Dylan R. Merola, 20,
of Rancho Cucamonga, California.

Marine Corps Lance Cpl. Kareem M. Nikoui, 20,
of Norco, California.

Navy Hospitalman Maxton W. Soviak, 22,
of Berlin Heights, Ohio.

Army Staff Sgt. Ryan C. Knauss, 23,
of Corryton, Tennessee.

Chapter 23

FAMILY REUNION

I'd often lay in bed and reread some of the message threads, stare at the photos that were sent, rewatch the video footage captured, and relive those two weeks in August 2021. I've been asked by reporters and journalists how many people I think I helped and assisted during the evacuation. And I can never give them the answer they want. Because for every Aishah and Huma, there were countless others that I knew I couldn't do anything for. And I can't even put a number on that either.

In the weeks after the withdrawal of Afghanistan was complete, I was in a fog. I was experiencing the very same feelings of hopelessness that I felt nearly a decade earlier while in a Syrian refugee camp. I wish that I could have done more but must live with the fact that there simply wasn't anything more I could do. I, along with hundreds and thousands of selfless individuals, did my very best to save lives, and that in and of itself should have been enough.

Then one day, Huma asked me if it would be possible to visit her uncle Mahmood and Sandara at Quantico. As the refugee camps were on military installations, I surely had the ability to go, but I knew access was probably forbidden. But…I also knew that other nonprofit organizations were helping at these sites, and with a little smile and some quick wit, I was sure it wouldn't be a problem to get in. Word of advice, it's always easier to ask for forgiveness than permission.

So, without much deliberation, I jumped in the car en route to the Marine Corps Base. Flying through I-395 and DC Beltway traffic, only stopping once at Target to get some toys, I couldn't get down there fast enough. I was excited and nervous at the same time, filled with the same feeling of butterflies you get on a first date.

Pulling up to the camp, there were signs everywhere saying, "Absolutely No Visitors." Shit. On the drive down, I had worked out this elaborate story that I was there on behalf of some organization for a meeting and was looking for someone named something generic. But as I walked up to the guard shack, with a duffel bag of toys, I figured I might as well level with them and tell the truth. So, I laid it all out.

"Hey, guys, I'm just here to drop off some stuff for a family I helped evacuate. They are in bay two, and I know, I know, but could you guys assist in getting this to them? They are toys for the little girl's birthday."

I was bracing for immediate rejection but instead got the most pleasant, "Absolutely, sir. I'll show you where it is." United States Marines... no greater friend today.

I texted Mahmood that I was walking up, and I could already make out what looked like the entire family waiting for me on the gravel road. Mahmood embraced me like a lost brother. The women nodded, and I put my hand over my heart acknowledging them, and then the children came over and hugged me. Okay, that's not the right way to put it. They hugged me, surrounded me, and then effectively tried to mug me. I can't blame them, though; I was carrying a bag full of toys. Mahmood shooed them away and invited me into his living area. An old World War II–era aluminum shelter that housed multiple families.

His English was decent enough for us to converse as he invited me to their new home—a makeshift bedroom partitioned with sheets and bunk beds. It wasn't comfortable or cozy, but it was safe and secure. His wife made us some tea, and we sat on their floor talking about things, all things: life, America, Afghanistan, and the future. Several of Mahmood's "neighbors" came by to meet me. The level of hospitality in that bay still amazes me.

I had only planned on staying for about an hour—long enough to give away some toys, meet the family, and be on my way back to DC. But after meeting everyone and handing out the toys to his daughters and Sandara—who, by the way, slept through nearly my entire visit—four hours had gone by in a flash. For some reason, I felt almost at home. I had a bond with Mahmood and his family that I couldn't put into words and not only because of our language barrier. A feeling like I was now a part of their family.

We continued to talk over tea as the sun faded and day turned to night. Over the course of my time with them, we covered nearly every topic of our limited conversational ability, but the one part of the conversation that sticks with me today was with Mahmood's oldest daughter. She was nearly twelve years old, and after I asked Mahmood about his work and what he was going to do now for a living, he looked at her and said something to the effect of her going to school and then becoming "a star." We laughed a bit, but then I pointedly asked her what she wanted to be. Her response: "an actress."

I looked at her and said that in America she can do that, and that she can be anything she wants to be. At the time I wasn't thinking about giving some altruistic advice or touting the greatness of America, but it was just an honest, candid response. And at that moment, I realized that had Huma not somehow connected to

David, had David not called me, had Huma not trusted me, had a brave army captain not taken a chance, and had some even braver soldiers not risked it all for this Afghan family, none of the hopes and dreams of Mahmood's daughters would be possible. It was at that very moment that I realized that the work that we did in those terrible few days was probably the most important thing I've done in my life.

Later that night, as I drove across the Memorial Bridge from Arlington, Virginia, to Washington, DC, passing monuments representing the best of America, a sense of solace came over me. The lyrics of Neil Young's song "Heart of Gold" pierced the cold winter night as I cruised with the windows down:

"I want to live
I want to give
I've been a miner
For a heart of gold
It's these expressions
I never give
That keep me searching
For a heart of gold"

Chapter 24

THE NEXT MISSION

My journey in life to this point has been anything but normal. I certainly have defied every piece of conventional wisdom and advice that I've received. And in doing so, every step forward has been met with one, sometimes two, steps backward. But whenever I've stumbled and fallen, I've gotten back up, and kept moving forward.

I've experienced the highest of highs and the lowest of lows. I've taken the road less traveled countless times, and in doing so have run into nearly every obstacle imaginable. I've battled demons and depression, been blinded by ambition, and mismanaged nearly every aspect of my personal life. I thought I climbed to the mountain top, only to realize it was a false peak. I've chased ghosts and dreams and recklessly thrown caution to the wind numerous times. I've seen the best of humanity and the worst. And I've witnessed triumph and despair. But in all these experiences, good and bad, for better or worse, they collectively brought me to this exact point in time.

Because on the cold winter night, I realized that in the four hours I spent with Mahmood, and after years of searching for something—a purpose, a mission, a place—I may have just found it. I had spent years trying to find a way to change the world. To make it a little bit brighter, so that when I depart from here and I am on my next adventure, I can say that I made it just a little bit better for the future. And in retrospect, I was foolish in thinking that.

As the clouds of emptiness that I had felt for so long lifted, I realized that I had been on a fool's errand. Because we can't change the world overnight. But what we can do is positively impact one person, providing compassion and care, showing love and support, and in doing just that we can and will change one person's world. It's as simple as that.

I pulled up to my house. Opening my front door to see George lying on the stairs above, I turned the hallway light on and walked up my old wooden staircase. As I leaned down to pat George on the head, whispering "good boy," in that exact moment, I realized that for the first time in decades, my heart was full, I was resolved, and I was content. And while I still didn't know exactly what I was looking for, or where this crazy journey called life was taking me, I felt that I was that much closer to finding it.

And as I finish this reflection of my journey to this point, what I can say with certainty is that this is not the end of my idealistic, sometimes quixotic, efforts to have a positive impact. In fact, it's far from it. Because for me it's time once again to get back up, dust myself off, put one foot in front of the other, and "Charlie Mike."